All My Relations

ALSO BY CHERYL WILFONG

Garden Wisdom 365 Days (2017)

The Real Dirt on Composting (2015)

Lost, but Found (2014)

Every Good Thing (2013)

Impermanent Immortality (2012)

At the Mercy of the Elements (2011)

That Rascal Mind (2010)

*The Meditative Gardener: Cultivating Mindfulness of
    Body, Feelings, and Mind* (2010)

Passacaglia on Passing (2008)

Off the Beaten Track (2007)

Scattered Clouds (2006)

*Following the Nez Perce Trail: A Historical Guide to the
    Nee-Me-Poo National Historic Trail with Eyewitness
    Accounts* (2nd ed., 2006)

Roasted Chestnuts (2005)

Hot Flashes (2003)

Light Fingers (2002)

India Journal (1999)

All My Relations

Cheryl Wilfong

HEART PATH PRESS
2017

Cheryl Wilfong

Cheryl Wilfong
Heart Path Press, L3C
314 Partridge Road
Putney VT 05346

www.cherylwilfong.com

All My Relations

Book design by Carolyn Kasper

ISBN: 978-0-9972729-5-6

Follow The Meditative Gardener _on Facebook_

Dedicated to the memory of

Margot Torrey (1928-2017),

in whose living room,

filled with treasures

from around the world,

so many of these essays were written.

Dear Friend,

Welcome to the 2017 edition of my collected writings—
memoir, travel, and essays, with Dharma permeating
all of it.

I didn't publish my little reflection books in 2015
and 2016. I was busy writing a breast cancer memoir in
2015. And in 2016, I tried out the idea, *Well, maybe I'm
done with those little books.*

But random people called me or emailed me or but-
tonholed me on the street. "Oh, I took your book out
of the library" (how did it get *there?*), "and I laughed
hysterically. I totally enjoyed it."

That's a good enough reason to keep publishing,
because Bill is still subject to pratfalls, we are still traveling, and I still love the Dharma.

As usual, the Warning Label reads:

— WARNING —

*You may think you know the characters in these writ-
ings, but if you ask the people with those names, you'll
hear a completely different story.*

Thanks to Mike Fleming, the editor of this volume,
who kindly pushes me to write more deeply and more
clearly and to finally write the endings to many of these
stories. I remain grateful to Jan Frazier and her writing groups, in which the first drafts of most of these
pieces were written. My critiquing group—Sarah, Sara,

Mary, and Melissa—keeps me on track. Jenny Holan, proofreader extraordinaire, scrubs my manuscript clean. (Oh! Does that feel good!) As always, deep affection and appreciation go to this book's award-winning designer, Carolyn Kasper.

Cheryl Wilfong
cheryl.wilfong@gmail.com

Contents

BILL

WHY I AM THE WAY I AM

LIVING GREEN

ALL MY RELATIONS

TRAVEL

BURTON ISLAND

ELEMENTS:
EARTH, WATER, AIR, AND FIRE

EXPIRATION DATE

BILL

Calamity Bill

I WENT ON A three-week retreat in March. Bill's life went to pieces. Oh, he carried on with his usual routine, while things fell apart all around him.

On Monday after I left, he went to the rehearsal with the Windham Orchestra, and at the end, his favorite yellow fleece vest from Eastern Mountain Sports was missing.

On the way home, he stopped at the dairy farm to pick up his weekly half-gallon of raw milk, which he carefully put next to him on the passenger seat. As he drove on into the March night, the milk jug tipped over and completely spilled out.

When he got home, he mixed himself a drink. He pulled out the ice-cube tray, which was stuck to two others underneath it, both of which dropped onto the floor and broke.

The next day, Tuesday, the new stove was delivered. Yes, it's cheaper to buy a new stove than to replace a $200 motherboard. They plugged it in. Meanwhile, Bill had to juggle having the gas company unhook the old stove, leave, and come back at the end of the day to hook up the new stove.

The electrician arrived with the wrong heater for the upstairs bathroom.

On Thursday, the generator maintenance guy showed up for his annual visit and fried seven circuits, the speakers on the computer, the router, the telephone, the modem, and the GFIs for the brand-new stove and the hot tub.

The bill for this service was $477—plus the recommendation to buy a new motherboard for the twelve-year-old generator. Bill didn't actually realize the circuits had been fried, because on Thursday he was playing celesta with the Windham Orchestra for their noon performance of *The Mother Goose Suite* by Ravel. During the performance, his sheet music jiggled and fell off the rack during his big solo, so he played with his right hand while he bent over and reached for the music with his left.

Bill had gone to great lengths to curry the favor of the orchestra's conductor by inviting his Rotary Club to have their Thursday meeting at the concert instead of the usual venue, the VFW.

Brattleboro Senior Meals catered the event, but Bill misplaced one of his eight sign-up sheets, so he had failed to order four lunches. Between the schools' concert at 9:30 A.M. and the community concert at noon, Bill zoomed over to his favorite deli, a mom-and-pop sandwich shop, to buy the missing meals.

When he arrived back at the theater, the Rotary members who were supposed to take the tickets from

Rotary members had not arrived. The Rotary lunches were not separated out. And the Rotary president didn't show up, so the Rotarians didn't know where to sit.

After the concert, the director of the Brattleboro Music Center dropped her purse and cell phone. He picked up her cell phone and went to give it to her. When he returned to the backstage area, his favorite fleece vest from Alaska, with a Tlingit raven embroidered on the back, was missing.

Once he arrived home, he realized he was without phone and internet service. The internet provider, Southern Vermont Cable, misplaced the order and didn't get back to him until the following Monday. However, the electrician—the guy who had had the wrong heater on Tuesday—came right over to inventory the fried circuits. This visit cost $251.

Bill called the generator company on Friday, but they wouldn't take responsibility for the electricity sizzle. "Sometimes the power spikes," they said.

On Saturday, he performed at the Celtic concert, which was emceed by his voice teacher, Jim. Bill sang two solos, but really, he was there to be the accompanist for eight other singers who had not rehearsed with him. He was chagrined to have to start one song over. Bill is, first of all, a performer. And for another thing, he couldn't find his reading glasses to see the music. He eventually found them on Monday—inside one of his organ shoes.

Well, that was the first week of my silent retreat-calm and peaceful.

Bill's Lost Glasses

WHEN BILL CAME home from church and told me he had lost his glasses, I only half listened because (1) Bill loses his glasses frequently, and (2) he always finds them—minutes, hours, or days later.

"I think one of the choir members must have picked them up by mistake, thinking the glasses were theirs," he said.

I've heard this type of story before; it's called *projection*. We all do it. Blame another person, and then the guilty party turns out to be oneself. Bill does what he always does: he called every member of his choir. He often practices organ at the Christian Science church because that's where he plays on Wednesday nights, but that week he also practiced at his Sunday church, the Congregational church. He took a flashlight and looked all over the organ and the chancel. He scoured the area again the following Sunday.

The following Saturday night, he dreamed that his glasses were in a rack of folding chairs. That third Sunday after losing his glasses, he looked again in all the usual places. Then he remembered his dream. He shook the rack of chairs, and his glasses fell to the floor. He recalled that he had hung his jacket on that very rack of chairs three Sundays earlier. His glasses must have fallen out but hooked themselves on a chair seat so he could neither see them from the top of the rack nor the bottom because they were lodged in the middle.

"Your unconscious came through for you!" I exclaimed to Bill.

"Possibly," he replied. "But I think it was God."

Billy's Bow Tie

Eighty-one-year-old Bill came down to the kitchen on Sunday morning, dressed for his job as church organist.

"Wook!" he said, pointing to his brown bow tie, perfectly tied around the neck of his tan shirt.

For a split second, I was magically teleported to a Sunday in Rumson, New Jersey, in 1939, when three-year-old Billy in his little suit rushed down to the kitchen before church to tell his mother in her Sunday dress to "Wook!" at his bow tie. Billy's forty-two-year-old father, just arriving in the kitchen with a twinkle in his eyes, looked over Billy's head at Mabel.

My now-silver-haired Bill said, "My father used to stand behind me as we both faced the mirror, and he taught me how to tie a bow tie. Now I can do it…"—and his hands finished his sentence with a flourish as he closed his eyes.

Beginning at age thirteen, Bill attended his father's alma mater—St. Paul's School in Concord, New Hampshire, where he wore a jacket and necktie every day of his school life. In fact, he was so habituated to this uniform that he continued to wear jacket and tie when he went to the New England Conservatory to study music. His classmates elected him president of the freshman class, mostly because he looked the part. However, as the younger brother in his family, he's generally much more of a follower than a leader.

"My father always told me to hang up my clothes at night. He'd say, 'No matter how plastered I am, I always hang up my clothes.'" And his father, Anthony Lispenard McKim, was plastered most nights.

Bill's older brother, Tony Jr., started mixing highballs for Billy when they were twelve and ten, respectively. Tony drank himself to death at age sixty-two, seven months after their mother died. He was found on a Wednesday, lying down on his made bed, dressed in jacket and tie, ready to go sing in Sunday's church choir.

Bill's the only one in his family of origin who isn't an alcoholic, but he does like his one drink of bourbon or scotch every night. His family ghosts—dressed for dinner in jackets and bow ties and speaking with an upper-crust East Coast accent—have been getting edgy as the sun heads toward the yardarm. When Bill pours his two ounces over the rocks, they can finally relax and smile.

Asking for Directions

E VERY TIME BILL wants to stop and ask for directions, I try to overrule him. First, I like to figure things out myself, and second, quite hidden from myself, I feel ashamed to ask, I feel ashamed not to know, I feel ashamed to reveal my temporary stupidity. Of course, these thoughts and feelings are all projections of my own self-judgments, because people actually love to be helpful and tell you what they know. These thoughts are just my inner child being afraid of my inner father.

I love figuring things out. When I travel by myself, I can sometimes go for days without conversing with anyone. I ask basic information questions, and that's all I need to know.

Bill is an ADHD guy, a slow reader, and he can be a bit slow on the uptake because his other sense channels are overloaded. As with anyone with learning disabilities, particularly those who grew up before the phrase "learning disabilities" even entered our vocabulary (in fact, before learning disability was recognized at all), he feels quite ashamed of his slowness and his inability to understand what's going on. But, quite often, the bright side of learning disabilities is that these people have learned to get their information in a different format—they have learned to ask; they have learned to relate to other people.

Bill doesn't read cereal boxes, and he doesn't read the notes I leave on the kitchen table for him. Reading is too much trouble. He would rather ask me for the information, the answer. He'd rather phone someone. He'd rather stop and ask for directions from a stranger. The thought of talking to a stranger makes me cower and cringe. *Oh no! Do I have to talk? Do I actually have to talk to a person?* I'd rather stay in hiding. I'd rather cocoon myself into the solitude of sudoku when I'm on an airplane. Bill would rather talk and joke with his seatmate. *Go right ahead, Bill. Just leave me out of this conversation.*

When we are in conversation with anyone, Bill needs to be in the middle. He cannot stand to be on the end of the table, on the end of the bench. He can't bear to be left out.

But after twenty-eight years, Bill has changed me. Now I sometimes talk to strangers. Now I sometimes ask for directions. I have to do this without thinking. I have to do it spontaneously. If I think about it, my intention grinds to a frozen halt. My history of reticence, shyness, bashfulness wins. I have to take a flying leap into conversation without remembering that I don't actually like to ask for things.

Maybe the directions I need to ask for are how to enjoy talking to strangers, just as Bill does.

Ready

"I'M NOT GOING to meet Ralph." I have to remind myself every time I start to hurry. Driving faster might save me one minute, but taking my foot off the gas pedal will probably help me drive more safely. Walking faster might save me a few seconds, but walking more slowly, sauntering, enables me to maintain at least a fraction of mindfulness.

Of course, I'm not going to meet Ralph. He's been dead for years. My father trained me well. "Don't be late." After years of trying, I am now no longer early. I usually arrive right on time, and I can even relax when I'm three minutes late.

Dad yelled at Mom because he always had to wait in the car for her to leave the house. Of course, she was the last one out of the house—she had just gotten four children ready to go.

I am so well trained that when Bill says, "Ready," I leave what I'm doing, put on my shoes, and am out the door within a minute. But when Bill says "Ready," he's got six more things to do: put on his shoes, find his glasses, pick up his wallet, and make a phone call. Meanwhile, I sit in the car waiting for Bill for at least two minutes, more likely five, and perhaps as many as ten. We drive down the road; we get to the second neighbor's driveway; and he remembers something he forgot, so we turn around and go back home to get it.

Not being late is part of my legacy from my grandfather, who died twelve years before I was born. He was a school bus driver with ten children. If one of them was late getting on the school bus—as Aunt Mary was, once, and only once—he'd drive off without her. He did not wait. My father hated waiting, too. I believed his threats that he would leave without me.

Once, when Bill and I were on a weekend bus tour to Montreal, my legacy got the better of me. The bus was supposed to leave at 10:00 A.M. to go to a nearby museum. I long ago opted to get on tour buses according to my own schedule instead of waiting for Bill and his schedule. I was on that bus at 9:55.

At ten o'clock sharp, the guide said, "Everybody here?" Bill was not, but I did not speak up. The bus drove the three blocks to the museum.

Bill has never let me forget that he *was* ready at ten o'clock, that the bus left early, and that he had to walk the three snowy blocks to the museum in his Birkenstocks.

So, I'm trying to retrain myself. When Bill says, "Ready," I sit down on the sofa and meditate. Within a minute, my relaxed mind remembers something that I wanted to take with me. Ready. On your mark. Get set. Relax.

Moving to Town

BILL SAYS HE wants to move to Brattleboro in a couple of years. He says his legs have about two years' worth of stairs left in them. When he gets out of bed, he has to set his mind to making his legs walk. This report from the future age-scape of the eighties comes from a man who swims four times a week, exercises with his TheraBands and does yoga most days, bikes two or three times a week, and hikes our nearby small mountains, gaining a thousand feet of elevation, twice a week. No matter how much effort he puts into exercising his body, though, gravity wins. No matter how much muscle building he does, the muscles atrophy, whether or not he wants them to.

Bill is tired of maintaining a house. He doesn't want to sit by and watch our house and gardens slide downhill—which is, of course, exactly where they are going despite all our efforts to the contrary.

Bill is much better than I am at calling the plumber, the carpenter, the electrician. I'd just let those things slide until the spirit moved me. Also, I hate to make phone calls. Bill's on the phone with his friends all the time, arranging bike rides or musical get-togethers. He nags me until I finally call the service person. After all, it's my house, not his.

I have to give him credit for mowing and pruning our landscape. But he's tired of spending three hours mowing our one-acre field and our lawn. This is a task he set for himself when he moved in with me twenty-eight years ago. If it were up to me, I'd just have the local farmer mow the field twice a summer.

I gave Bill a new chainsaw for his seventy-eighth birthday, and four years later he still uses it about once a week. Every year, he cuts five cords of wood for our two woodstoves. We have stockades of stacked firewood on the edges of our woods. He clears the trees that fall across the ski trails on the ninety acres of land we share with our neighbors.

I've bought in to the idea of "aging in place"—the ability to continue to live in our own home, our own neighborhood, our own community right up to the very end, even if it's just me by myself. Aging in place means making the house accessible now, before we really need it. I call the handyman to install grab bars in the bathroom. Fortunately, I designed my house so that I could live on the first floor in case I had a severe asthma attack.

I bought my land cooperatively in 1979 after two years of meetings with twelve friends. Since then, two men have died; there have been three divorces. A quorum of old friends remains in the nine houses on our private road—Partridge Road. I've known these people for forty-five years. Why would I leave them to move to town and run the risk of problematic neighbors?

Bill doesn't know about aging in place, and I don't expect Partridge Road is the place that he really wants to age into anyway. He's an extrovert. He needs town. He needs to be able to walk to his four concerts every weekend.

We each nominate our favorite options for the future. Bill wants to move to town; I want to stay here. Nowadays, couples have all sorts of variations on the theme of togetherness. One couple lives in a duplex so he can be sloppy while she is neat. Another couple lives ten miles apart—he in downtown Brattleboro, she in the woods in Putney—and, like best friends, see each other every day. Yet another couple has one partner who commutes to work two hours away and stays there during the week, while the other stays at home back in their house.

"Okay, Bill," I say. "You find an apartment that you want to rent." We are too old to buy another house; we want someone else to do the maintenance—we want the landlord to call the plumber, the painter, the electrician.

"And if you want to move, you have to start downsizing," I tell him. I say this knowing full well that it will take years for Bill to downsize. I am proceeding at my snail's pace—but it is, at least, some sort of pace. I take a box full of stuff to the swap program at the landfill every Saturday morning, and another bag of clothes and housewares to Experienced Goods every week. Recently,

Bill told me that his Rotary club was collecting fabric for the Pine Ridge reservation in South Dakota so that the women can make quilts. That gave me the opportunity to downsize my sewing closet. All that beautiful fabric went into a big clear plastic bag, ready to go to the Rotary Club meeting on Thursday.

Even though I bought a new sewing machine two years ago, I don't foresee any big sewing projects in my future, except for a summer quilt I'd like to make out of my grandmother's handkerchiefs. Hmm... I wonder if and when that will happen.

I started preparing for this aging in place by building an accessible guest suite attached to our two-car garage in 2012. I call it our old-age bedroom. "Bill, we can move into the bedroom in the guest suite," I say, but he can't imagine it. "There's no place for my clothes in that tiny closet," he says.

I *can* imagine sleeping in our guest suite—turning the living room into our bedroom and the bedroom into a very large walk-in closet.

Or, if we continue to sleep in the house, I can imagine a hospital bed fitting perfectly in the dining room, with a nice big window for watching the birds, and the toilet just a few steps away. I can imagine giving up all my houseplants and putting our queen-size bed in the solarium—glass all around. Or who needs a living room anyway? We could turn the living room into our bedroom. I spend most of my time in the kitchen, and Bill mostly lives downstairs in his music studio. We could have a caregiver live in the three rooms upstairs or in the guest suite, if we're not living there.

I do wonder what our relationship might look like if Bill moves into town and I don't. Maybe I would stay with him in his apartment on Friday and Saturday nights?

For now, it's all conjecture. Who knows how life will unfold? Bill-the-extrovert would do better in town, where he can be around people. I like living in the woods, surrounded by gardens, and walking to my morning meditation group of neighbors, which has been meeting for twenty-one years. I like our neighborhood potlucks. I like our neighborhood yoga class, which meets every Wednesday in the attic above my guest suite. I like camping with my neighbors at Burton Island State Park every August since 1988. Partridge Road has been my community for forty years. My neighbors are people I can depend on through thick and thin.

At some point, a next step will become clear, but for today, Bill fires up his chainsaw, and I go out to the garden. We continue our decades of parallel play in the landscape around our home, perhaps in preparation for a time of parallel living.

WHY I AM
THE WAY
I AM

Gift Giving

I SPENT MY TWENTY-FOURTH birthday in Hawai'i, where I was living with Uncle Harold, who had escaped our Hoosier homeland just two years previously. After we left my birthday dinner of lobster at the Pearl City Tavern, we stopped at a Kmart and looked over the decimated selection of live Christmas trees. Just think about how Christmas trees even get to Hawai'i. All that shipping means that Christmas trees, as well as every other thing brought to Hawai'i, are very expensive. In December 1971, Christmas trees on the Mainland were selling for $5, but in Hawai'i they were $15.

Not many trees remained at Kmart on December 8, and Unkies and I decided on a tree that had lost its top somewhere along the line—a real Charlie Brown Christmas tree. We took it to the checkout where the clerk said, "What a pathetic tree. Just take it." Unkies and I gleefully stashed our very first Christmas present in the trunk of his white Dodge Dart.

At this stage of his life, age forty-one, Unkies wasn't yet into the elaborate holiday celebrations he would host in his fifties and sixties. Fortunately, he did have a Christmas tree stand and one string of lights.

I was working as a bookkeeper and was saving money for a master's degree program. Not wanting to spend any money on decorations, I hung all the Christmas cards I received on the tree. I really loved that weird little tree; it was all mine.

My present to Unkies was a big tan terry-cloth towel, because he liked the feel of terry cloth. This was decades before big solid-color towels were in fashion.

On Christmas morning, we opened our presents. He gave me five bars of pink soap, a bag of chocolate chips, and a cookie sheet. At first, I was a bit disappointed. What kind of Christmas presents were these? But then I realized these were useful gifts. They were not disappointing gifts. In fact, this was one of the best Christmases of my life. I had such a good time with these ordinary gifts that, to this day, I've always included some useful little gifts among my presents to my family.

For a few more years I continued to buy presents for my long-distance family, but when I found myself still paying for Christmas presents on my credit card bill in February, I gave up on "real" (i.e., expensive) presents altogether.My sister and I agreed that stocking stuffers were the most fun gifts anyway, so we still give each other only little things.

Bill and I have almost stopped giving each other gifts, and that gives us a wonderful feeling of freedom. For his birthday, I did give him a bar of bicyclist's soap handmade in the San Juan Islands, where we took a bicycle vacation. I do like giving biodegradable gifts. On Christmas morning, we sit side by side on the sofa where we can look at the colorful lights on the Christmas tree and hold hands.

My brother no longer sends me gifts. He simply texts me photos of things he thinks I would like. Ahhh. What a relief that I can admire two dozen multi-colored gazing globes without having to actually figure out what I might do with one. Once in a while, I send him bacon-flavored dental floss or a Bo-Bo oat bar, since Bo-Bo was his childhood nickname. I like to give gifts like this—nothing that costs more than $10, and better yet, just $5. Things that cost more to mail than they are worth. We all already have more than enough stuff. A little trinket just says, *I'm thinking of you. If you don't like this, you can always regift it.*

You can call me a cheapskate—or you could call me a joy-seeker, because the joy of the gift is in the giving, not in the receiving. Sometimes people don't like the gifts they receive. They feel disappointed. Why would I waste money on an expensive piece of junk?

What's the purpose of a gift anyway? It's a way to say *I love you* or *I'm thinking of you* or *I just* had *to buy this gawd-awful thing for you.* Does a bigger gift mean bigger love? Do more gifts mean more love? According to the Beatles, "money can't buy me love." I take their message literally. Five bars of soap and a bag of chocolate chips told me that Unkies loved me, even though he would never say such a thing.

I refuse to give obligatory gifts, opting instead for the practice of tough love, which is more in line with my values than subsidizing white privilege—even though I myself am the beneficiary of such privilege. I watch friends cave in to the emotional blackmail of you-owe-me or you're-supposed-to-give-me-a-gift. One friend forked over a thousand dollars for her distant grandchild's summer camp and received nary a thank-you. Even a thousand dollars couldn't buy that grandmother an expression of the love she craved from her dear ones.

Since I so seldom receive thank-you notes from youngsters, I have set my gift-giving limit to age18. I then send the eighteen-year-old a note saying that I will no longer send gifts if I don't receive a thank-you. Nowadays, a text or an email suffices, and it doesn't even have to literally say "thank you." I am happy to receive a little update on their life. Otherwise, I feel I am sending gifts into the void. *Yoo-hoo. Does anyone out there even care if I send a gift?* I do love you, but I need some mutuality in this relationship. Otherwise, even though we may be related, we aren't really relating to each other.

Once, on a retreat, I offered the buffet table of lunch to a Buddhist monk who can only eat food that someone gives him. Even though I was standing ten feet away from him, I was practically bowled over by the wave of gratitude he exuded. The lesson I learned in that moment was to practice gratitude, even for things I don't particularly want. I want to simply appreciate the person who thought of me, no matter how small or useless or ugly the gift may be.

There's the joy of giving, but, there's also the joy of refraining from over-gifting, especially in our materialistic, consumerist society. I once asked a ten-year-old about his recent birthday gifts as he was just putting the finishing touches on his brand-new Lego pirate ship. "Oh," he sighed. "I prefer experiences to presents."

I echo the sentiments of that wise boy. Especially with our loved ones, we are seeking the experiences of caring and appreciation, but money can't buy me those expressions of love and acceptance.

Having a Drink

Leaves get yellow.
The tree puts out fresh roots
and makes them green.
Why are you so content
with a love that turns you yellow?
— Rumi

AFTER MY MOTHER died of alcoholism, I stopped drinking. Just stopped. The stopping surprised me. I had considered taking the fifth Buddhist training precept, "refraining from intoxicants," for a few years, but I couldn't see my way clear to actually refraining altogether. I had given up hard liquor; that was not hard—I didn't like the taste. I had given up wine because I couldn't remember the names; I knew that if I really liked what I was drinking, I would remember its name. That meant only beer remained on my menu, and I definitely remembered those names and enjoyed the taste of beer.

My beautiful, but yellow, almost green, mother died of a liver that had turned into a rock (cirrhosis). Alcohol had already robbed her of the feeling in her feet (neuropathy), and she shuffle-walked with a wide stance. Her digestive system had been giving her warning signals. Then she fell into a hepatic stupor as her liver failed. She was seventy-four when she died. Only seventy-four. She died three weeks after her younger sister, my dear and fun Aunt Jenny—also a drinker—age seventy.

Alcohol not only stole a quantity of my mother's life, it also dissipated her quality of life. Alcohol withered her God-given talents of art, interior design, and money management. Her natural grace shriveled into bitterness when she drank. Her poise turned into stumbling. All her beautiful possibility come to naught.

After she died, I lost my taste for alcohol altogether. My desire for a drink was simply gone. Gone.

Some people assume I'm a prude because I don't drink. I find I cannot talk about abstinence, even with social drinkers, without raising their hackles. I cannot tell them a single thing about how the world looks from a sober and clear-minded perspective; they are simply not interested.

What's the difference between being a prude and being prudent? I have had the repeated experience of alcohol dimming my emotions as much as twenty-four hours later. I don't have full access to my feelings the day and night after I've had a drink the evening before. The long-lasting numbing effect of alcohol is not ordinarily perceived and astounded me when I finally noticed it with focused mindfulness in my weekly therapy group.

Nowadays, mindfulness is so important to me that I

do not understand why anyone would want to anesthetize their emotions every evening of the week with a glass, or an entire bottle, of wine, unless they are self-medicating.

The statement of the fifth precept ranges from "keep my mind clear" to "I vow to refrain from intoxicants that cloud the mind and lead to heedlessness." The things that intoxicate us nowadays range from a bag of cookies to drugs to addiction to our iToys. Name your poison.

There's a reason intoxicants are called "poison." They are toxic, after all. But even before intoxication, alcohol loosens my intentions to follow the other four precepts:

1. Do no harm to anyone.
2. Take nothing that is not freely given.
3. Use my sexual/sensual energy wisely.
4. Speak truthfully and helpfully.

The precepts angle us toward a life of integrity. Someone who lives with integrity is a trustworthy person. Would you trust an alcoholic with your life? How about someone behind the wheel who's drunk a six-pack of beer or a bottle of wine? I don't trust my life to someone whose blood alcohol level is "only" .03, which is to say one drink. The legal limit for many states is .08. Some countries have a zero tolerance, and many countries have a legal limit of .05 or less.

Alcohol leads to heedlessness, and this heedlessness makes us careless about being kind. Everyone laughs at the butt of a joke, for instance, and the butt laughs too to show what a good sport he is, even though his feelings have been hurt. If that's "fun," I think I'll abstain.

I feel very grateful to friends who don't try to push a drink on me or belittle my sobriety with comments like, "What's the matter with you? Can't you have a little fun?" As if having fun is dependent on alcohol; as if nondrinkers can't have fun. As if the word *toxic* isn't hiding in the middle of the seductive word *intoxication*. I've seen the *toxic* part up close and personal; I wouldn't wish that on anyone.

A little alcohol loosens the slight tension of social anxiety, so that people can schmooze with each other and enjoy each other's company. I watched a Board of Directors I was on having pre-dinner wine. Since we didn't really know each other, people spent twenty minutes talking about wine in order to have a common topic of conversation and feel comfortable with each other.

As a writer, I sometimes notice the presence of a silent character in the room: her name in Wine. Wine whispers seductively, *Drink me. Drink me and show how chic you are. Drink me and show how smart you are. Drink me and show how beautiful you are.*

At a greeting card store, I recently saw a card: *Wine: It's how classy people get drunk.* Wine or beer—it's how people I love ruin their health. It's how a secret message is installed in the younger generation who is silently watching every move their parents make: getting inebriated is normal, feeling tipsy is fun, and more is better.

The thought that stresses me is that alcohol is as

harmful to your health as cigarettes, yet alcohol is so much sneakier than tobacco. Medical research shows that one drink a day is good for your health, but I am so seldom among drinkers who have only one drink that I am surprised when my hosts stop after their first drink. Much more often, the people I am around have a before-dinner drink, wine or beer with dinner (possibly two glasses), and a post-dinner drink. And then, since there's just a little bit left in the bottle, just finish the bottle. Why not?

Some heavy drinkers hide behind the camouflage of social drinking, as my mother did. But if you have to drink to be social, that's not social drinking. If you have a drink by yourself, that's not social drinking. If you're drinking more than two bottles of wine per week, that's not social drinking.

"For God's sake, Mildred," my dad would say, "take just one drink."

She couldn't. She couldn't "just say no," as Nancy Reagan did. But then, Betty Ford could not just say no either.

I follow the A.A. teaching:

The first drink, a woman takes a drink.
The second drink, the drink takes a drink.
The third drink, the drink takes the woman.

"Oh, a little drink never hurt anybody," my mother slurred.

I didn't believe her, but other members of my family tree did. And so, the plague of alcoholism and addiction continues—in one sibling and several of my very dear nephews and nieces. They are not bitter drunks as my mother was. They are just sociably soused and having a good time. And hey, what's wrong with that?

Why, oh why, my beloved ones, are you content with this love of alcohol that will turn you yellow?

Girls Against Women

In 1975, when I was in my late twenties, I corrected my language and stopped referring to mature women, including myself, as *girls*. In 1988, when I pointed out to my evangelical brother that he referred to the men at his office as *men*, and he called the women *girls*, he made an immediate course correction. The men all had their own offices; none of the women did. Each woman shared an office with one or two other women.

Nowadays I hear women in their mid-thirties refer to each other as *girls*, and it breaks my heart.

A newborn baby boy is called "my little man." Have you ever heard a baby girl called "my little woman"? More likely, she is called "baby girl" (notice the lack of the word "my"). Men are men from the day they are born. And girls are girls until... when?

My parents' generation, the World War II generation, called each other girls and boys. The boys came home from the war. Even in his seventies, my dad would say to his crew of hay-balers, "Well, boys, I've got to leave you now. I'm tuckered out."

Boys and girls morphed into *guys* and *gals* in the 1950s. My mother called her friends *gals*. Although I refuse to use the word *girls* to refer to a woman over the age of sixteen, I find myself using the word *gals*. "See you gals later." Sigh. I'm still not happy with my choice of words.

The possibility does exist of redeeming the word *girl*, and I hold out some slight hope for that. When we were hiking Mount Mooselauke one August, we met a fifty-year-old woman from Georgia, through-hiking the Appalachian Trail by herself. I asked her what her trail name was. "Saybak," she said. Before she left home, she went out drinking with her women friends and toasted them, saying, "See all you bitches at Katahdin" (S.A.Y.B.A.K.). She wasn't so sure her friends would actually be there to meet her at the end of the A.T. Nowadays, some women—urban women, young women—call themselves *bitches*, as if that word can be redeemed. I hope they are right.

Girls don't want to be women. They hate women as much as men do. Oh, it makes me cry to write that, but I've discovered my own wormhole of misogyny. It started out consciously enough: *I don't want to be like* **them**—my aunts and my mother gathered in the kitchen before and after holiday dinners cooking, slaving away for the do-nothing men in the living room watching a football game on our black-and-white TV. No, I did not want to grow into that narrow definition of the 1950s homemaker.

When I was a senior in college, in 1968, the dean of women recommended I read *The Feminine Mystique* by Betty Friedan, and that book changed my life for the better. I gave it to my mother, and it made her bitter. She felt powerless, still locked in a patriarchal marriage for another twenty years. Divorce was a terrible stigma before no-fault divorce became widely available in the 1980s. Women could not get their own credit cards until the 1980s. My mother's credit cards were all in the name of Ralph Wilfong, and she always signed the credit slip "Mrs. Ralph Wilfong," as if she had no identity of her own.

In 1970, I became a full hairy woman when I stopped shaving my legs and underarms. Today's girl-women even shave their pubic hairs in an effort to continue to look like hairless girls. At least, that's the message the media gives us. Big, strong men want to make love to childlike "girls." They do not want women. Just feel how distasteful the word *woman* feels in your mouth.

Teenagers starve themselves in their vain attempts to continue to be Mommy and Daddy's little girl. They are fighting their own bodies. Oh, so sad to witness that external battle of the sexes internalized in a young woman who is fighting reality with all her might. Feminine hygiene products are now called "girl products," though I've never met a girl (a female under the age of menarche) who uses them.

My seventeen-year-old granddaughter worked on a lobster boat in Maine one summer and was called a "bait girl." When her thirteen-year-old brother did the exact same job, he was called "third man."

Meanwhile, despite being called "girls," young women give up their toys and take on care-giving skills—baby-sitting and cooking—while so-called "men" keep playing games and buying bigger and bigger toys until "he who dies with the most toys wins."

Girls, little girls, are sexualized at a younger and younger age, so that anorexia now begins at age seven. A six-year-old thinks the new realistic Barbie looks fat. The five-year-old is instructed how to stand in a photo so that she looks thin. The one-year-old is photographed in her undies with bunny ears and her lips in an O, looking oh-so-cute and like a miniature Playboy bunny.

Oh, my breaking heart.

Speed Dating: Twenty Years in Twenty Minutes

WHEN I WAS sixty-seven, I went to a personal growth workshop, and for one of the exercises, the group of 200 divided into women and men. The women, about 140 of us, stayed in the hotel conference room, while the sixty men went to a smaller room to receive their instructions.

We women, standing in a large circle, were told to remain in our circle when the men came in. Each man would approach one woman, look into her eyes, perhaps hold her hand or give her a hug. We asked our nervous questions.

I could feel what a perfect petri dish this was going to be for my own wallflower-ness. Although I am not, in Bill's words, "a professional wallflower," I was already predicting my failure at this exercise, as if by expecting the worst, I would be pleasantly surprised if something else, anything else, happened.

The blonde woman next me, in her late forties, was having a fit of anxiety. "Oh, I can't do this," she said to her other neighbor, a slim, dark-haired woman in her late thirties. The instructions were that if one of us felt overwhelmed by a man's attention, we could step back, and our sisters beside us would close the gap, thereby protecting the overwhelmed one. The thirty-ish woman assured the Nervous Nellie between us that we would protect her. This was a silent exercise; no talking.

All questions about the exercise answered, the lights in the room were lowered; soft music began to play; the door opened, and in walked the smiling men, who immediately scattered all over the room.

If I'd been paying close attention, I would have felt the tension of desire and resistance, wanting and not wanting, looseness and tightness in my body.

One man made a beeline for Nellie, and I watched as she looked into his eyes and embraced him. Then they stood looking into each other's eyes. After a minute, the instructor softly said, "Woman meets man. Man meets woman. Change."

All the one-minute partnerships dissolved, as the men backed away and sought new women. Once again, Nellie was chosen, and just as I was trying to figure out a story about her, I was chosen by a six-foot-five, barrel-chested man, by far the biggest man in the room. He reached down to hug me as if he were well practiced with short women. I noticed I did not rise up on tiptoe to meet him, but stayed grounded, flat-footed—*sure*-footed—on the floor. Just as I was about to create a story about this, the instructor's voice said, "Woman meets man. Man meets woman. Change." I gazed into my temporary partner's eyes, and he walked away.

And so it went. In about twenty minutes, twenty years of my dating life unrolled before my eyes—ages twenty to forty. If the phrase "twenty years of dating" makes you cringe, I can assure you it was worse than that.

Nellie was chosen by men repeatedly. I was chosen about half the time. The young woman on the other side of Nellie was not chosen at all, until one man broke the mold and hugged one woman, then her neighbor, then the next neighbor, then the next until the minute passed, and it was time for change to happen again.

All those years of being a single woman, flagellating myself for being single. *What is the matter with me? There must be something wrong with me.* Comparing myself to all the Nellies I have known whom men are attracted to. I have my stories now: *They have pheromones. I don't.* Or: *They know how to connect and bend to a man. I don't.* Or: *They were molested as children, and men are unconsciously attracted to them.* I didn't use to be so sure of this last one until Bill repeatedly confided in me the various women he was attracted to. Time after time, it was a woman who had told me she was sexually abused as a child.

Really, what's the use of comparing myself to other women? My aloneness was a gift, though I never saw it that way. It was a time when I could pursue my many different paths without trying to drag someone else along with me, someone who would most probably have his own ideas about direction.

Chosen. Not chosen. Connected. Unconnected. Free. Freedom.

When I was chosen by a man, I could see my own familiar responses. Happy equality with the big bear of a man. Feeling dismissed by the man who hugged each woman in turn. Trying to cling to the slender (probably gay) man with cold fingers. Being too forward with a hesitant man. Wanting. Not being in sync. Constantly trying to adjust myself to fit my him of the moment.

After twenty minutes or so, we were released from the man-woman container, free to walk around and meet (silently) and embrace anyone in the room—man or woman. Free to smile and meet at our own natural pace. Neither too much nor too little.

You could say this wisdom comes too late. I needed this insight twenty-five years ago, forty years ago. I could have used this wisdom when I saw that the men I dated married the next woman after me—ten times in a row—and I tortured myself for being so incapable as a woman.

All the while, I have many women friends who are never chosen or have been chosen once, but not again. Some women get an early start; I was rather late out of the starting gate at age forty-one, but still not as late as my sixty-five-year-old friend, married for the first time, or an eighty-year-old friend married after fifty years of singlehood.

My path looks like no one else's, and even though those others looked as if they were on the same path with each other—married right after college, perhaps, or in their twenties or in their thirties—so many are now divorced. They are now single, and I am surprisingly coupled.

It turns out that everyone has a different path as man meets woman, woman meets man.

Change.

LIVING
GREEN

Running on Sunshine

WHEN BILL WASN'T looking, I bought a car. A three-year-old used car. A 2012 Nissan Leaf with 7,600 miles on it for $13,000. I thought that was a good deal, since the new 2015 cars cost $20,000 more than that.

We have fifty-nine photovoltaic solar panels on our roof, so we produce more electricity than we use, which nets us $450 a year. In 2013, I missed the opportunity to receive the credit in cash, so now it gets complicated. We could form a "group" with one of our neighbors, so they would pay their monthly electric bill to us instead of Green Mountain Power. My own to-do power sank to nearly zero at this thought. I called the installer, Integrated Solar, and the receptionist said, "Buy an electric car." That sounded so much easier.

It took me a few months to follow up on that idea, what with surgery and radiation. But then, I just happened to drive by the Nissan dealer in Lebanon, New Hampshire. I turned around, parked, and walked in. Yes, they had one used Leaf, and it was silver—one of our acceptable colors. The new ones I had seen in Keene were charcoal or red, not colors I care to live with for the next ten years.

Bill wasn't all that keen on the idea of an electric car. "Wait until the battery storage improves," he said.

"They say that the average driver only goes thirty-two miles a day," I said. "The Leaf can go eighty miles. I really think that's plenty for us."

We were early adopters of the Prius. Bill was still driving his 2001 model—the very first Prius. Then, in 2005, we bought a second Prius for me. At the time, it seemed a radical idea to be a two-Prius family, though it quickly became quite ordinary. Ten years later, we have photovoltaics on the roof and geothermal heat from our well water in the basement; evidently, I like the idea of being an early adopter. I bought the Leaf.

Bill signed on as co-owner. (Much easier in the event one of us dies.) A week later, he told me he wanted to pay for half of it. He sold his old Prius to a college student, because he was head over heels in love with the Leaf. I was so thrilled with the Leaf that I went to the local print shop and asked them to make a bumper sticker for me: *Running on Sunshine*.

In the first month we put 1,000 miles on the Leaf, just running back and forth to town. We average about 10,000 miles a year. That's 10,000 miles of running on sunshine. No petroleum products. None. No oil changes. No tune-ups. No lube jobs. That's somewhere between 200 and 335 gallons of gas that we are *not* buying. We are not paying Saudi Arabia or a fracking oil company in order to fuel our car.

The dashboard readout tells us that we are getting four and a half miles per kilowatt. I'm mystified by this measurement. I can't picture it in my mind. I have a sense of how long a mile is, but how big is a kilowatt? One kilowatt from Green Mountain Power costs about sixteen cents. So each mile "costs" less than four cents.

My 2005 Prius averages about forty-five miles to the gallon. Gas prices are exceedingly low now—let's say, $2.25 per gallon; so my fuel costs are five cents a mile now, but it has been six cents a mile in recent memory. Our truck, which gets about thirty miles to the gallon, costs more than seven cents a mile for fuel. Then there are all the service costs of an internal combustion engine—including two or three oil changes a year—that we do not have to pay, because the Leaf has an electric motor.

Bill and I no longer have his and hers cars. We now have the long-distance car (my Prius) and the short-distance car (the Leaf). Every day is a day of negotiation. "Where are you going? And when?" This mode of communication and relationship is new to us. Of course, there are bumps, and lots of compromising because we both love the Leaf and each other.

Bill feels so happy to have lived long enough to drive this car. With all the Leaf's bells and whistles (including a heated steering wheel for winter!), he feels that he has entered the space age. He spent a month reading the various manuals that come with the car. The Leaf does have a bit of a Jetsons feel. It's silent, and it has great pick-up. Best of all, it's teaching me to be a safer driver. I actually stay within the speed limit in order to save battery power.

I went ahead and bought a car without Bill's agreement, and now we are both very, very happy.

Trash Diary

I KEPT A TRASH diary one week—just to be mindful of how much stuff I recycle or throw away. We have four feedbags for recycling stuff hanging in the woodshed: two for paper, one for glass bottles, tin cans, and #1 and #2 plastic. The fourth bag is for food packaging—all the plastic containers of hummus, yogurt, cherry tomatoes, which I reuse as pots when I'm dividing plants in the garden to give away.

That week I kept the trash diary, as happens every week, the heavyweight winner is junk mail and recycled paper. I usually open envelopes from nonprofits in hopes of scavenging a sheet of paper with a blank side from all that paper that comes with a request for my money.

If the letter has a blank side, I place it in a box under my kitchen desk. If, perchance, the envelope has a stamp on it or doesn't have a SKU code at the bottom, I save it in a cut-down cereal box. Later, when I need an envelope to pay a bill, I reach into that box and get one—no matter the size. Using recycled, free envelopes, I haven't bought a box of envelopes in years. My kitchen-desk drawer has three sizes of labels; I stick one of these over the address of the charity, and then address the envelope in my own handwriting to whomever I'm paying the bill to.

The printed-on-only-one-side paper eventually goes upstairs into a box under my printer. As a writer, I'm always printing off pages and pages of essays, which I later edit while I'm sitting on the living room sofa. For every ream of printer paper from Staples, I probably go through two reams of reused letter paper. Eventually the reused paper does hit the wastebasket.

Bill is the main recycler in our house, so he often empties the overflowing trash basket from my office into one of the feedbags that hang in our woodshed. He hauls those bags to the town recycling bins about every two weeks.

As for plastic bags, I wash them out after every use and stash them in a bottom drawer in the kitchen. Eventually, a hole develops, and then they go into our bag-of-bags—a big clear trash bag in the woodshed, which we fill up with used plastic bags. When it's full, Bill takes it to the supermarket recycling program.

Fortunately, Vermont has the five-cent return policy on bottles and cans (though not all of them), so Bill also returns those to the grocery store.

Meanwhile, despite all the recycling, we've collected a grocery bag full of trash—mostly food packaging, about one bag a week. We throw that into the neighborhood dumpster shared by the ten households on Partridge Road.

Reduce. Reuse. Recycle.

Burning Trash

WHEN BILL AND I went to Costa Rica in 2003, I overheard young tourists gasping at the sight of local people burning trash in their yards. "Don't they know it's bad for the environment?"

I grew up with a fifty-five-gallon trash barrel in the back yard. Taking out the trash meant taking it out to the barrel, striking a match, and setting everything on fire.

My Hoosier cousin who is a farmer still does this. After a picnic, he burns the paper plates and paper cups. Of course, paper plates are now plasticized. I think long and hard about whether to tell him about dioxin in the soil. His mother had breast cancer a few years ago. I can't positively say there's a causal link, but dioxin and cancer are linked in my mind. First of all, burning the chlorine bleach that makes white paper white releases hydrocarbons into the air. Then there's that thin plastic coating.

When I went to the Republic of Georgia to visit my friend Nancy, her Georgian friend Tamara drove us to a village to visit some friends. The April day was chilly, and we sat in a small, south-facing, glassed-in porch that had a tiny wood stove for warmth. I bit my tongue as I watched the lady of the house throw a two-liter soda bottle into the flames of the stove.

Burning trash may be bad for the environment, but what else can you do with trash if you don't have a trash service and a landfill nearby?

Not until I was twenty-five and sharing a house did I become acquainted with the idea of a trash service. We'd leave a black plastic trash bag with a dollar bill on top beside the driveway, held down by a rock. When we woke up the next morning, the bag and the dollar were gone. One housemate postulated that Mr. Whipple, who supposedly came to pick up our trash, was actually a raccoon. Who could say anything different?

My uncle in Waikiki thought that Hawai'i's garbage should all be thrown into a volcano. That politically incorrect idea would surely exact some retribution from Pele, the fire goddess, who still breathes and walks among the islands. Just ask the locals. Even I know a story of someone who actually picked her up as she was hitchhiking on the Big Island. She sat in the back seat, chain-smoking, and then disappeared like a puff of smoke.

In the town of Hveragerdi, Iceland, located on top of a magma chamber, the residents used to throw all their trash into a local steam vent. One morning they woke up to find that the earth had burped during the night, and their trash was now scattered all over town.

Our town of Dummerston, Vermont, had the opportunity to become the site of an incinerator that would burn the trash for our county. The NIMBY backlash trashed that idea, so now our county hauls its trash to Rutland on the other side of the state, an hour and a half away.

No one wants their own trash, or anyone else's, either. Just throw it away. But where is "away" anyway? A long, long way away. Out of sight, out of mind. But the problem is, we are running out of trash sites, and our "away" is someone else's backyard.

The Great Pacific Garbage Patch is the size of Texas. Micro bits of plastic now cover the floors of the all the oceans. When Bill and I took a walk on a Nature Conservancy beach in Molokai, the sand was thickly littered with plastic of all descriptions. Everywhere you look, you can see that we are trashing our environment.

No matter how far away you throw it, you can't get away from trash.

Used Books

I WRITE A BOOK of memoirs every year and give it to family and friends. It's a collection of short stories that people say that they keep in the bathroom or that they read just before bed. My friend Vera emails me to tell me that her copy of *Impermanent Immortality* fell into the toilet and had to be thrown away.

I imagine all of my books eventually being thrown out in the trash. What else can you do with used books nowadays? Even the library has given up on their annual used book sale. I was dismayed to see twenty boxes of leftover books sitting under the eaves of the Putney Public Library being rained on, four months after their Memorial Day book sale fundraiser. Now I see why. No one wants them.

To whom can I give my used books? These are books I have enjoyed or books that have provided useful information to me. I would like for someone else to read them. The hospice thrift store has way too many. I see boxes of books sitting outside near the back door at a quarter apiece, and still no one wants them. I take some books to the swap program at the landfill in hopes that someone will find my donated book on their burgeoning bookshelves of giveaways.

We have entered the age of throwing books away by recycling them with the junk mail, but I can't bear to throw a book away. It feels like blasphemy. I have visited schools in India and Myanmar and Zimbabwe where an entire class of fifty students shares one book. Where can I give my books to people who need them?

I box up stacks of books and send them off to a literacy program, Reader-to-Reader, which stocks libraries in disadvantaged schools and communities. I live in a community where most people have advantages—the advantages of downloading a book on a Kindle or borrowing books from a good library, which has a decent budget for new books.

Of course, I wouldn't have boxes of used books if I didn't keep buying books—from so-called used book websites, of course. I say "so-called" because most of the "used" books I buy are actually brand-new. Even though I never order a hard-copy book from Amazon—because of the Walmart way they treat publishers such as myself—many of the used book warehouses are owned by Amazon. As hard as I try, I cannot escape the strangling tentacles of Amazon. Of course, when I buy books for my Kindle app, I *have* to go through Amazon. The advantage of a Kindle is no used books and no recycling. No resale either, so Amazon gets all the money.

For those who cannot break their addiction to

Amazon, at least you can put your used books into an Amazon box, download a shipping label from Amazon, and send the box off to the nearest Goodwill, and Amazon pays the postage.

Mostly I buy Dharma books, but I do keep a few novels on hand for vacations. You might tell me to go to the library, but I don't read a book within two weeks. Or maybe I like the piles of books by my bedside?

As a lifelong learner, I have been an avid reader since age five. I've mostly forgotten the titles of the thousands of books I've read, and I certainly don't recall their plots. You could say my "inner library" has been washed away by time, although I assume the effects of all that reading are stored somewhere in my unconscious.

It seems a pity to throw books into the recycling bin, yet perhaps the Information Age is teaching me a hard lesson. In one sense, every book I've ever read has been a virtual reality that I have enjoyed. Yet the reading of the book, the comprehending of the book is an evanescent as a memory—here this moment and gone the next, the memory glimmering in and out of existence until it fades altogether. All the books I've ever read are only dim memories at best. All those unremembered titles are gone.

The hard-copies of books serve as a reminder of my past good reads, but, truthfully, when I close any book, I almost never look at it again. So, I may as well recycle my old books to make more paper for more and newer books.

Prevent Cruelty
to Animals

I RECENTLY SAW A bumper sticker that read: *Prevent cruelty to animals. One meal at a time. Vegworld.com.* Since another bumper sticker on the same car said *I love my pets*, I wasn't surprised. Yet another bumper sticker said *Cattitude*. But that combination of messages gave me pause. Did the owner of this car have a vegetarian cat? Was her cat preventing cruelty to animals? Maybe it did not go outdoors and kill a few hundred birds a year. Maybe it stayed indoors and hunted mice? Or maybe her cat ate only kibble, and she never opened a can of cat food, not even when her kitty wasn't feeling well? Kibble ingredients include meat byproducts and rendered fat.

I wonder how a meat eater, such as a cat, feels about a vegetarian diet. If my sweetie is at all representative, he gets so hungry for meat that he's just got to fry up an organic burger or a little steak from the local beef farm. I, the cook of the family, am never hungry for meat. I'm perfectly content with seven vegetarian dinners each week. I don't notice the absence of meat. To keep the meat-eater of the household happy and for my own self-protection, I do buy chicken once or twice a month, and fish just as often. Although I grew up with half a beef in the freezer and hamburgers every Saturday night while the adults were having steaks, I can no longer bear the smell of beef. Sweetie can cook his own burger; I'm not touching it.

You may think I am splitting hairs when I say that I do like ground bison. Mostly I use it for chili or goulash. I wouldn't chow down on a bison burger though, because it's too much meat at one sitting.

I'm still trying to imagine a vegetarian cat. Or a cat that prevents animal cruelty. Being allergic to all critters myself, I didn't realize until just a few years ago how cats can maul their prey. The cat may call it fun, but it looks like torture to me.

Okay, so let's imagine a vegetarian cat who never goes outdoors. I wonder if its claws have been removed so that it won't shred the furniture. The owner may think that this is now a civilized cat, but I'm betting that it's salivating as it watches the birds at the bird feeder through the window.

Cattitude. Does this mean feeling grateful for your cat? Or does this mean that you yourself have the attitude of a cat? I'll let my own catty attitude show with these examples of a dog's diary and a cat's diary.

DOG'S DIARY

5:00 A.M.   *Going outdoors. My favorite thing.*

5:10   *Coming indoors. My favorite thing.*

5:15   *Taking a nap. My favorite thing.*

7:00   *My owner gets out of bed. My favorite thing.*

7:10   *Dog food! My favorite thing.*

7:30   *My owner takes me for a walk. My favorite thing.*

Et cetera

CAT'S DIARY
Day 983 of My Captivity

My jailers think they are being cute when they harass me with the name "Kitty," a name that I detest. I sometimes manage to surreptitiously scratch them with my claws, just to remind them that I am carrying weapons—a fact my stupid captors fail to notice.

If I can escape, I boast about how strong I am by leaving a headless mouse or a dead bird at the front door of my jail cell. When they are repelled, I know I have accomplished my mission.

Cats and dogs are predators, whether or not their owners want them to be. An animal is simply living out its animal nature. A cat is not preventing cruelty to animals. What we humans call cruelty, a cat or dog calls the law of the jungle. My neighbor's eighteen-year-old cat went out to hunt every night. One morning, Pandora didn't come home. My neighbor looked out her front window and saw a crow who had something white in its beak. Dear Pandora, the predator, had become prey. Her hunter's spirit was being passed on into the chain of life.

Of course, human beings know better than to be cruel, though we may be unkind, hateful, or vengeful to each other in any number of ways, small or large. As my Burmese friend, Koko, said so succinctly, "We are not animals." We have the opportunity to live by the Golden Rule and embody our full humanity. We have the opportunity to prevent cruelty to all animals, whether or not they are humans.

Leaving Things Better Than I Found Them

O N T H E W A Y out the door one morning, I spilled granola on the floor. I was already a minute late. My first thought was "Later. Leave it. I'll clean it up later."

Then I recalled my New Year's resolution to leave things better than I found them. I sighed. I got a brush and dustpan. I walked out the door another minute later. A couple of stray oats still lay on the floor. I still wasn't leaving that floor better than I found it.

At our New Year's Eve sit at Vermont Insight, I always ask people to write down a resolution. What are you resolving for the new year? What are you intending? This is one opportunity to really focus on changing your karma a little bit with that new intention, that new resolution. I wanted to focus on my intention to leave things better than I found them.

Bill and I are avid recyclers. Feedbags that used to hold a hundred pounds of oats are hanging up in our utility room: two for paper and one for both plastic and glass. I have another feedbag for the many food containers that I can reuse for potting up plants.

I take my best-quality clothes and housewares that I'm not going to use anymore to Experienced Goods, the thrift store run by our local hospice. I deposit my so-so stuff to the yellow Planet Aid box, to be sent to some Third World country. And I take my usable junk to the swap program at the landfill on Saturday morning. I love the swap program, where I can find all the plastic flowerpots I could ever want; I bring home one or two dozen every week, so I can pot up my divided perennials and give them away. Giving things away can be one example of leaving other people's gardens better than they were.

In a recent Vermont Insight newsletter, one fact struck me in particular: each dollar you spend for new stuff represents about a pound of carbon dioxide emissions. This is just another reason for me to continue shopping at Experienced Goods.

If we really want to clean up the earth, recycling begins at home. And I can tell you from experience that this connection between my actions and saving the planet is difficult to make.

I live with a dumpster diver on a private road of ten households. The ten of us share one small dumpster, which is emptied every week. Bill and I take our plastic grocery bag of trash there about once a week. If Bill finds cardboard cartons in there, or any of a variety of other things, he'll retrieve them and take them with him on his weekly trip to the recycling bins in Dummerston Center, 1.5 miles away from our house, and about 1.2 miles away from the dumpster.

Bill has offered to pick up people's recyclables, but no one calls to ask him. He even buttonholes one or two neighbors, who smile, but never call him.

What are some of the reasons why people don't recycle?

- I'm too busy.
- I don't have the time—to wash out the containers or to take them where they're supposed to go.
- I'm confused. What goes where?
- I forget to recycle.
- It's not convenient. It's out of my way.
- It's messy.
- My trash doesn't make a difference.

I am talking about an attitude shift here. If we want to save the earth, how about starting with our tiny corner of it? The world is a mess, and it feels as if it's becoming more so as environmental rules and regulations are repealed in favor of rampant capitalism.

My sphere of influence is very small, yet I can make a tiny difference. My desire to change the world comes down to this: I want to leave my corner of the world better than I found it.

ALL MY
RELATIONS

I Love to Pay Taxes

SITTING IN THE airport one evening in 2016, I couldn't help but see Donald Trump on the TV monitor, and, unfortunately for me, read what he was saying as it ran across the bottom of the screen. "I hate how the government spends our taxes."

Well, it's true that I don't like paying way too much for the defense budget. But what I think of more immediately are the services of Medicare and Social Security, which I love and am entirely grateful for. I love the highways that I drive on. I love the fact that people obey the rules of the road, thanks to various police departments. I love the airplanes that fly me to my brothers in Indiana or my sister in Idaho. I love the flight controllers and the paved runways. I love the weather reports, which I check two or three times a day. I feel so grateful for the way our taxes are spent on these things.

I especially love our national parks and our park rangers and the employees who manage our national forests and the government lands that aren't beautiful enough to be parks. Sure, there are mistakes and glitches and loopholes, and ranchers and oil companies exploiting federal lands, but these federal lands are our national treasures, and thousands of people spend their lives protecting them.

I love how my little town of Dummerston spends my property taxes—paying mostly for the schools but also for road maintenance so that I can drive my car safely on the winding East-West Road or any number of dirt roads, no matter the weather. The highway guys are out there snowplowing, sanding, and salting in the dark of winter, grading and re-graveling after mud season, and mowing roadsides in the summer. Thank goodness! I do not begrudge paying school tax in our town, even though I have no children. I went to a public school for twelve years. I graduated from a state university, paid for by the citizens of Indiana. Unknown people paid for my education. Now it's time for me to pay it forward.

I actually love paying taxes to the state of Vermont. I trust our legislature to spend money conservatively and wisely on all manner of human services. I don't begrudge a single penny that I pay to the state.

Of course, investigative reporters shine a light on the dark corners where government services fail to meet the need. Bill's award-winning journalist daughter in Boston wrote an article about the lack of autopsies on babies and children who have died under suspicious circumstances. The state of Massachusetts doesn't have the money, doesn't have the taxes, doesn't have the common wealth, doesn't have the people power to pursue the suspects. There are hundreds of sad stories like that. Underfunded by taxes, state agencies limp along as best they can, serving the disadvantaged. We are caught in a bind: we want the government to provide services, but we don't want to pay the taxes that fund those services.

Have you noticed that while we are distracted by the word *taxes* (and we each have our own opinions about government and taxes), we are in fact being invited to hate. If first we hate how the government spends our taxes, then it's a very short step to installing the habit of hate in our heart and hating people we don't like and then hating groups of people who are different from us. Do I really want to hate all the civil servants who are doing the best they can to serve me and three hundred million other Americans? Can we hate the civil servants, hate the government, and yet love our country? If we hate the government, does that mean that we hate the people we just elected to office? That doesn't make sense.

Hate doesn't make sense, but it feels great to have the adrenalin of a rant against the government (or those who govern) coursing through your veins. Hate, however, is not good for your heart. Hate's close cousins, hostility (toward the government, for instance) and resentment (of political leaders, e.g., "I hate Obama.") are the best predictors of heart disease. So why would you want to practice hostility—toward the government and taxes, toward Black Lives Matter, or toward Muslims? You're just hastening your own heart failure. We could even say that hatred and hostility are a failure of the heart.

I choose love because love trumps hate. Just ask your deity. Can you simply waltz through the Pearly Gates carrying the habit of hate in your heart?

All religions have a version of the Golden Rule: *Do unto others as you would have them do unto you.* This bleeding-heart liberal (C'est moi.) has deeply believed in the Golden Rule since childhood. I am convinced that what goes around comes around. This time around, I am very fortunate—through no doing of my own. I want to set up the circumstances for fortune to smile on me tomorrow and on my deathbed, and then for whatever happens when I see those Pearly Gates. That means building habits of love, kindness, and compassion right now.

We are all *ubuntu*—linked together by our common humanity. That's why I am happy to pay taxes into the commonwealth that is our country.

---

* *Ubuntu* is a South African Bantu word meaning "I am what I am because of who we all are."

All My Relations

W<small>E HAD BEEN</small> on a water fast for forty-two hours when our retreat of 200 people was dropped off in a city park in Santa Cruzada on a Saturday afternoon. We had no money, no cell phones, no credit cards, no I.D., no water bottles, and our instructions were to maintain silence with one exception. We could say, "I'm hungry."

The downtown park had the usual assortment of street people, drunks, people off their meds, and homeless people living on the sunshine of Southern California.

I felt a bit weak and woozy from lack of food, as I walked into the hundred-foot-wide strip of park on the top edge of the Palisades, on the west side of Ocean Avenue. To the west, and 200 feet below, lay a wide beach and the Pacific Ocean rolling in; to the east, downtown Santa Cruzada.

Many retreatants walked toward the pier, but I headed north. After a block, I sat and rested on a park bench. Five minutes later, I recognized a water fountain. Ahh! Water! Dear water was the only thing I could use to fill up my empty stomach.

Then I felt the urge to pee, so I walked down the

staircase in the Palisades, across a walkway overpass above the Pacific Coast Highway, and onto the beach where a block of toilets sat. After relieving myself, I washed my hands, and there in the sink were ten blueberries. Maybe someone was rinsing them, and these escaped? I ate them. My first food in 43 hours. They tasted utterly delicious. Bliss.

I was huffing and puffing by the time I climbed the stairs back up to the park, and I soon sat down in the shade near a white man using a laptop. "I'm hungry," I said. He looked at his watch. "Yes. It is time for lunch." It was 2:00 in the afternoon.

After a while I moved on to a black man with a plastic bag—of food, I hoped. I sat near him, and he offered me the rest of his cheesy pasta from California Pizza. Normally I don't eat wheat, and I avoid cheese and dairy products, but food, any food, fit the bill. "You've got to give back," he told me cheerfully. I still hadn't said a word. Then he thought he wanted a few more bites of his pasta, which I handed back to him, and he handed it back to me for the last five bites. Same fork.

As part of this retreat, I had just worked on my prejudice, my fear, really, of black men. One of the things I had said to the other person in my dyad was that "black men shouldn't be so forward." Yet, at this minute, how deeply thankful I was for this man's forwardness! Beliefs really are so useless.

After a while I walked on and soon sat down beside a large black woman who asked me questions. Bound to silence, I could only smile at her. She offered me an apple. A golden delicious. Every bite was heavenly. I felt well satisfied. She gave me half a banana. Then a handful of lime-flavored tortilla chips, which I savored. I felt she was treating me like I treat the birds who come to our bird feeder. (I often put out a handful of sunflower seeds on the deck rail for the joy of seeing chickadees, goldfinches, and woodpeckers.) She was feeding me a handful at a time to keep her company. To top it off, a Nips, a hard caramel. I took my time with each bite, so she finished a large bottle of V-8, which she waved at an old Native American–looking man who was sorting through nearby trash cans.

"I see you here every Saturday and Sunday," he said to her, and she nodded. "Yep. It's paradise."

She got out her knitting and told me she had just taught herself to knit from YouTube videos. I reached for the hat and showed her an alternative way to hold her yarn. Then I corrected a couple of her dropped stitches. After a while, she gave me a small ball of pink yarn and some straight knitting needles, so I began a narrow, ruffled scarf.

We knitted companionably for forty-five minutes, and then she began to pick up. I wrote the instructions for the ruffled scarf on a piece of paper and gave it to her.

It was almost time for me and my fellow retreatants to convene at the meeting place for the end of this three-hour exercise, so I began walking south. I passed a man standing behind some shrubs, smudging a young woman with burning sweetgrass. After she walked away, I walked around the shrubs and offered myself to him. He told me he was a Tlingit shaman from Alaska, down to collect the body of an elder, a ninety-eight-year-old woman. It was very expensive, getting all the paperwork done to arrange for the shipment of the body.

I pulled my empty pockets inside out. He smudged me anyway, waving the smoke of the burning sweetgrass around my head, arms, torso, and legs as he chanted in Tlingit, and ended with the English phrase "all my relations."

Yes, all the people here in this park were my relations. The homeless, the writers, the lonely, the crazies, the grieving, the ones too busy to notice, the givers, the walkers, the runners, the babies, the old, the fat, and the skinny. These are the people who took care of me in a time of need.

All my relations.

Exodus to Shanghai

B ILL AND I were in Marfa, Texas, having a personal tour of Museum 98, a building that had been the officers club at Fort Russell during World War II. German prisoners of war from Rommel's Afrika Korps were housed there in West Texas from 1943 to 1945, and two of the POWs painted desert-scenes murals in the U.S. Army officers' club that today is called Museum 98.

The conference room had a display of Holocaust material, including a book entitled *Exodus to Shanghai*. I ordered it online before our guide finished our tour.

One of my meditation teachers, later known to the Buddhist world as Ayya Khema, spent nine years in Shanghai, from 1940 to 1949. In her autobiography, she describes such an interesting life that Shanghai is only a single chapter.* She arrived as a seventeen-year-old unschooled Jewish teenager named Ilse Kussel and left as a married woman with a two-year-old daughter. *Exodus to Shanghai* gives the larger context of the 18,000

---

* *I Give You My Life: The Autobiography of a Western Buddhist Nun,* Ayya Khema. (Shambhala Publications, 1997).

Jewish refugees who lived in Shanghai before, during, and after World War II.

Jews trying to escape Germany after Kristallnacht in November 1938 had very few choices. The United States had strict limits on Jewish immigrants (about 16,000 a year), and other Christian countries similarly did not want Jews. Meanwhile, though, the Chinese consul-general to Vienna was handing out visas to everyone who applied. With a Shanghai visa in hand, people were permitted to spend a week applying for a passport marked with a "J." Jews could take 10 marks ($4) out of the country with them. Relatives from elsewhere in the world might send money, but sometimes the distant relatives were unresponsive.

After Kristallnacht, Ilse's parents booked passage for her on the Kindertransport—ships going to the United Kingdom in March of 1939. They themselves were able to escape to Shanghai in late December 1938. Ilse's father had been one of seven brokers on the Berlin Stock Exchange. Would-be émigrés could pack a roomful of furnishings under the watchful eyes of the dreaded secret police, the Gestapo. By the time they got to Shanghai, their stuff might or might not arrive. Nevertheless, for the first three years after Kristallnacht, 18,000 Jews from Germany and Austria were able to develop a vibrant subculture and essentially trade their pfennigs back and forth with each other.

Meanwhile, in Britain Ilse was assigned to a Russian Jewish family in which she was expected to serve as nanny to their several children. Having had a posh childhood, Ilse didn't even know how to boil water. She was unhappy with her adopted family. In early 1940, at the age of seventeen, she boarded a ship bound for Shanghai in order to join her parents.

Jews from Baghdad had settled in Shanghai a century earlier, and some of them, such as the Sassoon family, had become quite wealthy. These Arabian Jews funded soup kitchens and offered aid to the incoming European Jews. Most of the Jews who arrived in Shanghai between 1937 and 1940 were professional people—there were many doctors, for instance—with very few other marketable skills.

The Japanese were not anti-Semitic. Even when the Gestapo arrived in 1942, the Japanese refused to give in to German demands to put all the Jews on a boat and sink it at sea. The story goes that when the Japanese commander of Shanghai asked, "Why do the Germans hate you so much?" the leader of the Jewish community said, "Because we are short and Oriental." The Japanese had no quarrel with the Jews, but when it came to the Chinese, they could be quite cruel.

In early 1943, all "stateless persons," meaning all European Jews, were ordered to jam themselves into the Shanghai slum of Hongkou, along with the thousands of poor Chinese who already lived there, in an area three-quarters of a square mile in size. With several people crammed into every room, the ghetto subsisted for the next two and a half years, until the end of the war.

About 10 percent of the Shanghai Jews died while they were in China; the survivors were forced to emigrate once more. After the war, and even after the Holocaust had come to light, the United States still had very low immigration quotas. In 1946 and 1947, only a few hundred Jews left Shanghai for the United States. In 1948, President Truman increased the quota to 200,000, and a thousand Jews immigrated every month from China, escaping just before Mao Zedong's forces arrived in Shanghai in 1949.

Just as I finished reading *Exodus to Shanghai*, my local rabbi asked if I would light a candle at the interfaith service of remembrance in late April. Of course, I said yes.

Only when I arrived at the Yom haShoah service did I realize the ceremony was a remembrance of those who had died in the Holocaust. There were eleven candles, one for each million of the eleven million who perished in the Holocaust—six million Jews along with five million Roma, gays, Blacks, Slavs, Jehovah's Witnesses, prisoners of war, the mentally ill, and the physically disabled.

I lit one candle silently, in memory of my dear teacher, Ayya Khema, and all the other Shanghai Jews.

TRAVEL
Dedicated to Susan Ross
7 February 1946 – 17 May 2017

Renting a Car in Greece

I HANDED OVER MY credit card and driver's license at the car-rental desk at the Athens airport, and Bill laid down his driver's license beside mine.

The young man behind the counter started typing in information from my IDs. Then he picked up Bill's license. "How old are you, sir?" he asked.

"Seventy-eight," Bill replied, keeping to himself the fact that he was only four weeks away from seventy-nine.

"I'm sorry. sir," the clerk said. "We don't rent to anyone over the age of seventy-five. Insurance. You know."

Ouch! I'm only eight years away from seventy-five myself. And then what are we supposed to do? Hire a guide? Go on tours?

On the one hand, I'm happy to do most of the driving. When Bill drives in a foreign country, we're both anxious; when I drive, he's the only one who's anxious, and I am relieved to be in control.

Still, I do like sharing the driving. Usually, Bill and I trade off every hour or so, but if one of us loses alertness, we will even trade every half hour. I drive in the early mornings; he drives late at night.

So this trip was all on me. Yes, it was Greece. Bill

could drive. No one was looking. And maybe no one even really cared. But I don't like cheating, no matter how good an excuse we have.

It's not that Bill's a good navigator, though he can be if he focuses. Mostly he's sitting in the passenger seat, looking out the windshield, surprised by every new sight. This is aging adult ADHD, with the emphasis on "distracted."

Thank all the Greek gods and goddesses that Siri has arrived via my iPhone. She tells me what to do, and Bill confirms it. Or more likely he asks me what to do when he has difficulty reading the GPS.

"I don't know, Bill. You're the navigator. You tell me what to do." I can't look at the phone while looking at the Greek stoplights, which are small, and the only signal for the intersection stands at the corner beside Bill. In other words, I have to crane my neck to see the basic red-yellow-green small-town stoplight. There are no frills like a stoplight on the far side of the intersection or hanging in the middle of the intersection—stoplights you can actually see. No super-sized American stoplights. Just a single two-foot-tall stoplight from the 1950s.

Fortunately, Siri saves both of us. "In one point two miles, turn left."

Oh, you should hear her pronounce long Greek words without the slightest hesitation. I have no idea what she's saying in all that jumble of thetas and chis and sigmas and upsilons. She pronounces the Greek words in a speedy, unremitting American accent. I could have sworn that she said lake-on-a-kiss when it looks like Lakonakis.

I chauffeur Bill all over the Peloponnese for two weeks—Athens and Sparta, Corinth and Kalamata, Epidaurus and Olympia. Just Bill and Siri and me.

Siri

———

WHEN SIRI IS good, she is very, very good indeed, but when she is bad, she is horrid.

Last fall, Siri directed me faultlessly over hill and dale in central Vermont, on one dirt road after another. An hour and a half later, when I arrived at my destination in Calais, Vermont, it felt like a miracle.

Then one summer day, I asked her to take me to the lawyer's office in Lebanon, New Hampshire. Two months previously she had taken me there—exactly there. But that day, Siri was quite mischievous. I should have known something was wrong when she told me to get off at Exit 19. *No, no,* I thought. *I'm sure it should be Exit 18.* But I humored her and drove through the poor, not-much-is-happening downtown of Lebanon. Siri kept wanting me to go south of the interstate, though I knew very well that the lawyer's office was north—right next to Dartmouth-Hitchcock Medical Center.

Finally, I pulled over and called the lawyer's office to say I was late, thanks to Siri, and I'd be later still, now that I was following my nose instead of that bad, bad girl, Siri.

Bill's Enhanced
Driver's License

J UST DAYS BEFORE we left for our Big Bend vacation in late March, Bill lost his driver's license. "How are you going to get on the airplane?" I groaned. "Use my passport," he said. "And who's going to be driving the six hours from El Paso to Big Bend?" I asked. "Well, maybe they won't let me drive anyway because I'm over seventy-five, like Greece," he said.

Fortunately, we live just three miles from a DMV office, a sub-office actually, which is open three days a week. Bill went and got himself a new license—the free kind.

The license that Bill lost was an enhanced driver's license. Since both our licenses expired in November and December 2015, we trekked across the Green Mountains to the other side of Vermont to buy enhanced driver's licenses at $25 each. In fact, we drove to Bennington twice, because the first time we drove that winding hour-long drive over the mountains, we arrived just as the only staff person who could issue enhanced licenses was taking her lunch break at 11:00 A.M. Then at 12:30, the computer system went down before our numbers were called, so we drove home empty-handed.

The second time we tried, I managed to get Bill out of the house early, so that we arrived at the Bennington DMV early. Did I mention that all the DMVs where you can get an enhanced license are on the other side of the state? Bennington, Rutland, and Burlington. Also Montpelier, our state capital, in the center of the state—two hours away from us.

The second time, it didn't take long for us to walk out with our hot-off-the-laminating-press precious enhanced driver's licenses.

An enhanced driver's license enables us to go to Canada, Mexico, and the Caribbean without a passport. Supposedly. Two months later, in early 2016, we went to the island of St. Lucia, taking our passports as well as our brand-new driver's licenses. The airline wasn't accepting enhanced driver's licenses yet, and when we returned, passport control wanted to see our passports. Hmm.

A year later, we spent our winter vacation in West Texas, hoping to see the desert in bloom. Big Bend refers to a big bend of the Rio Grande. It's the bingo wing on the west arm of Texas. Big Bend National Park is in that triangular dip, with Big Bend Ranch State Park just west of the national park.

One of the first things you notice about the Rio Grande is that you can wade across it. It's not really that grand a river. What's grand about it is that it's almost 2,000 miles long, the fourth longest river in the United States.

The Mexicans call it Rio Bravo. You might think that's because it takes courage for illegal immigrants to scurry across the blistering Chihuahuan desert of southwest Texas for a hundred miles before blending in to the great American melting pot. But in the nineteenth century, the illegals went the other direction. Texas slaves escaped to Mexico, which abolished slavery in 1828.

Bill and I first glimpsed the Rio Grande in El Paso, where we were stuck for a day, waiting for our queen-size suitcase with hiking poles and hiking boots to catch up with us. The local Delta office was very accommodating, giving us vouchers for lunch, dinner, and a hotel. The next day, on our way out of town, we followed the Mission Trail, a series of missions that were built on the Rio Grande in Mexico between 1680 and 1790. The Rio Grande has changed course, so that now three of the five missions are located on the Texas side of the river.

With all the political talk of building a wall, I wanted to go see the 200-mile long section that was built ten years ago between El Paso and Ciudad Juarez, which, with a population of 1.2 million, is twice as big as El Paso. Five blocks away from Ysleta Mission (the oldest of the missions), I pulled off onto the dirt beside an on-ramp to Interstate 375, and even before I opened my car door, a Border Patrol SUV with flashing lights pulled up behind me. A helicopter rotored overhead.

"Oh hi," I said to the heavy-set young man in a brown uniform, brown cap, and sunglasses. "We're from Vermont, and I wanted to see the border. Can I take your picture?"

No, I couldn't take his picture in front of the wall, but I could take a picture of the wall and the back of his head with his cap that said U.S. Border Patrol on it. The wall is actually a twenty-foot-tall fence that you can see right through, though we couldn't see the Rio Grande from our vantage point slightly above the river. El Paso sucks up all the water in the river, but the flow is replenished by the Rio Conchos, which flows into the Rio Grande from the Mexican side 200 miles downstream.

After that excitement, Bill and I continued southeast on the Mission Trail to see the other two missions, and finally on to Interstate 10 to Marfa, Texas, three hours away. The next day, we dropped down to Big Bend Ranch State Park and spent the day driving the fifty-mile river road along the Rio Grande, stopping to see geology, historical sites, and flora, and then taking a nature walk. I kept remarking, "That's Mexico over there," in order to make myself believe it. Those cliffs were Mexico. That riparian marshland was Mexico. That desert was Mexico. All looking pretty much the same as the Texas side, and not looking like foreign territory at all.

On our first full day in Big Bend National Park, we drove down to Santa Elena Canyon for a half-mile hike into the canyon. Fifteen hundred feet of rock cliffs towered above us on both sides. We waded across the river to a sandbar on the Mexican side. They're going to put a wall here? Where? A third of a mile above our heads? I couldn't see a wall making any sense, except as a boondoggle.

The next day, we drove down to the river again, forty miles farther east. The temperature was a sweltering 105 degrees, and Bill wanted to take a hike. "No, Bill," I said. "It's too hot for me to hike. I'm taking my enhanced driver's license and going across the river to have lunch in Mexico."

Bill dropped me off at the border crossing. I pushed through a turnstile, walked down a path, and stepped into a rowboat. One minute and $5 later, I was in Mexico. Did I want to walk the kilometer to town, or ride a horse, or ride a burro, or ride in a truck? Each option cost $5. I chose the truck option, and my truck driver/guide Lázaro dropped me off at the only restaurant in the town of Boquillas, a pueblo of about 300 people. At 2:00 in the afternoon, I was ravenous. Furthermore, I assumed that my mission to Mexico was to spend as much money as possible in the local community, which, due to its location, is essentially exiled from its own country. Most supplies come into town the same way I did. It's easier to get food and gas (in red five-gallon containers) from the United States.

As I was eating a large portion of guacamole, I overheard a customer say, "You've got a bigger menu than you did the last time I was here, a few years ago."

"Oh, yes," the proprietress said. "Now we have

electricity, and we can do a lot more. There's a solar array on the other side of town."

After lunch, I asked Lázaro to take me to see the solar array: eighty-one panels of photovoltaic solar energy that brought this town into the twentieth century, about a hundred years late. Thanks to electricity, people can now stand outside the little grocery store and use their cell phones to access the internet. Otherwise, only one landline comes into town, and you have to make an appointment to use it.

Lázaro showed me the church, the elementary school, the kindergarten, the clinic. The crafts were either primitive embroidery or beaded scorpions and ocotillo cactus. I picked up one beaded roadrunner, and the old man who was selling it told me that the bird is called *el paisano* in Spanish, meaning "countryman" or "from the same country." I was feeling that way myself about the border with Mexico.

I returned to the United States very happy with my two-hour cross-cultural excursion to Mexico, which added the state of Coahuila to my list of the fourteen Mexican states I've visited. Bill felt happy about his hot hike.

By the way, ten weeks later, Bill needed something from the junk drawer in the kitchen, a drawer we open several times a day to get scissors, charging cables, screwdrivers, stray batteries, or the big box of matches we use to light the wood stove. When he opened that drawer, he found his long-lost enhanced driver's license.

Where's My Daypack?

A<small>T</small> 7:55 A.M. we were at the Atlanta airport walking through the TSA precheck line, which snaked back and forth a dozen times. "Aren't we supposed to be in the precheck line?" Bill asked.

"We are," I replied, thinking, *even though this line looks like one at Disneyland.* The precheck line at Hartford, where we usually fly out of, is normally quite short. We had stood in that line the previous afternoon. Then, since Delta had changed flight times on us, we elected to spend the night in Atlanta rather than try to make a connection with only a thirty-minute layover in the extensive six-terminal Atlanta airport. Thanks to Hotwire.com, I had booked a room at the Westin for $72.

"Where's my daypack?" Bill asked.

I looked at him. He had his roller bag and his tummy pack, but he was right—he wasn't wearing his daypack, and he was looking frantic.

"I'll take your roller bag," I said, "while you go look."

He started swimming upstream through the snaking line of precheck people behind us. But no, he hadn't put it down on the floor.

"Did you leave it on the hotel shuttle?" I asked him.

"No," he said.

I dialed the Westin anyway. This is one of the miracles of smartphones. Mine remembered the number I had dialed last night to ask for a shuttle pickup. "We were on the 7:40 shuttle," I said. "Did you find a daypack?" The hotel clerk said, "The 8:00 shuttle just left. Let me call the shuttle driver." While I was on hold, I said to Bill, "Let's go back out to the shuttle island and wait for the shuttle to come by again." After holding for four minutes, I hung up and called back.

"What color was your daypack?" the clerk asked.

"Navy blue."

"And what brand was it?"

"Bill, what brand was it?"

Bill had that harried look, which means that his mental clutch is in. His short-term memory is unavailable; his long-term memory is unavailable. He is stuck in the present moment of high anxiety. "I don't remember."

The shuttle arrived a few minutes later, and Bill was reunited with his daypack.

I often say that Bill is a somatic guy. His body acts out his emotions, particularly when he's too ashamed to express them out loud. It's also a way for him to disagree with me, the alpha in our little family. The undercurrent of Bill's message to me was: *See? We could have taken the 8:00 shuttle and gotten here in plenty of time.*

And my unstated message to him was: *Isn't it good we took the 7:40 shuttle so we have a cushion of time in case anything goes kerflooey?*

As it turned out, we were both right.

Flying at Different Altitudes

I OFTEN SAY THAT Bill and I live in different time zones. I wake up at 4:30; he wakes up at 8:30. I eat an early lunch; he eats lunch as late as possible. Even though I call him to the dinner table at six, he doesn't arrive for fifteen or thirty minutes. If we're going somewhere together—say, a 7:00 movie—I want to leave home at 6:40, but he's not ready to go until 6:50 or even 7:00. Et cetera.

So we live in different time zones, and now I have incontrovertible proof that Bill and I fly at different altitudes. On our last trans-Atlantic flight, we each had our own TV screens turned to Flight Data. As we descended into Boston, my screen consistently showed that I was flying a couple of hundred feet below him, even though we were sitting side by side.

Yes, I know that the data on our screens was refreshing itself at different intervals. Still, I like the metaphor of flying at different levels. Particularly when we're making transitions, as we often do when we travel, I'm usually in the lead while Bill is floating somewhere in the space between where we've been and where we're going. He's enjoying the process, while I'm headed toward the results—airport, gate, airplane.

Just twelve hours before we landed in Boston, we had been in an Underground station in London waiting for the Piccadilly line, which was delayed. As the sign flashed TRAIN APPROACHING / STAND BACK, we saw a work train rumble by with open carloads of rock, trash, tools, and equipment. After a few minutes our train arrived, then came to a standstill two stations later. Looking at the handy Tube app on my iPhone, I could see that we could switch to the Bakerloo line, which I could hear rumbling above us, and go to Paddington.

"Let's change," I said to Bill, who was still digesting the standstill. We were headed to Heathrow and losing precious minutes of the half-hour cushion I had built into our journey. This is one example of how Bill and I fly at different altitudes: I calculate backwards from our destination and add a cushion; he calculates assuming everything will happen as it's supposed to, and decides he'd rather have an extra twenty minutes of sleep. Thankfully, I had prevailed that Wednesday morning.

We trundled our roller bags off the Piccadilly line, by this time following a stream of other desperate roller bags. I followed the signs for Bakerloo to Paddington, which Bill could not distinguish in the hubbub of too many things happening too fast and way too early in the morning.

Upon our arrival at Paddington Station, we studied the signboards for Heathrow Connect and three minutes later boarded a high-speed train to the airport. Oh, I do love a public transportation system, especially when it works despite various hiccups. We arrived at Heathrow at seven, just as I had planned, although we had come by a more circuitous route.

Why is it that the kiosk always spits out my boarding pass and then refuses to cough up Bill's? Why is it that even though we're in the security line together, I'm recombobulating and waiting on the other side for five minutes before Bill makes it through? I'm racing with time while Bill bumps along, chatting with everyone he sees. Never in a hurry, he's never aware of the time, since he has no internal clock. We're not only in different time zones, we're flying at different altitudes, and moving at different velocities. Together.

Meditating in Yangon

I N   M Y   T W E N T I E S , I wanted to travel the world and to speak many languages. Now, I'd rather stay home, but I don't refuse travel opportunities that come my way.

I used to want to see the sights, to expand my vision, to broaden my horizons. And I do love every country, every state I visit. I enjoy the change of perspective that enables me to see life from another point of view, a new place where things look different, where even the language assumes something different from the American English that warps my own view of so-called reality. Obviously, my view of the world is true. So think seven billion people. Seven billion views. Seven billion worlds.

I have the great good fortune to be able to say "Yes" when the door of opportunity opens. When my neighbor Connie said, "Let's go to Burma to meditate," I said "Sure," even though I was unsure of what, exactly, that meant. I had traveled with Connie on her annual work trip to Thailand and Laos once before, and I knew that surprises often happened in her company.

So we traveled halfway around the world until we were twelve and a half hours away from our home time zone. When the sun set in Burma, it was rising on the same day in Vermont.

Once we arrived, it turned out that Connie had too much work to do. As the senior program officer of an NGO, she didn't have time to meditate. She needed to visit projects in other parts of Myanmar with the country director. So I chose to spend five days at an easy-to-get-to retreat center on the outskirts of Yangon, where a Dharma friend often stayed on her annual visit to Burma.

The abbot, Sayadaw U Indaka, instructed me to watch my breath rise and fall at my abdomen during each hour of sitting meditation followed by one hour of walking meditation. A brown *longhi* and a white shirt was the uniform for all laypeople—male or female. I was given a brown Burmese *longhi*—a skirt that was actually a length of cloth. I wrapped it around my waist and tucked it in, and found I needed to redo it every forty-five minutes or so. The women also received a brown sash to wear Miss America–style over the blouse. This neatly covered both breasts. My sash sagged and fell off my shoulder, so I folded it and wore it over one shoulder like a baby's burping towel.

Going on retreat is what many Burmese do for their vacation. They don't go far away from home; they can't. Until recently, a Burmese passport was good for only one year, and it took hours and even days of standing in line and filling out forms to receive one. Now, their passports are good for three years.

But the Burmese can't travel in their own country if they don't have the proper paperwork. Imagine being confined to Vermont and applying for a paper that would allow you to go to New Hampshire. How would one ever even get to the airport in Connecticut, two states away?

As a foreigner, I was supposed to have a special meditation visa, but my tourist visa had to suffice. It took three weeks for the embassy of Myanmar to stamp my eight-by-eleven-inch application for a tourist visa and staple it into my passport.

The particular retreat center I attended had two meditation halls: one for the Burmese and one for the foreigners. Foreigners included a handful of Americans, some Europeans, several Malaysians, and a sprinkling of Chinese.

The statue of the Buddha in the foreigners' meditation hall sat on a stage in front of a mural of a purple flowering tree with a river flowing by. Birds and animals and butterflies sat in the tree or on the ground. I love dioramas, and this one was particularly beautiful.

The Buddha in the Burmese meditation hall sat on a table, surrounded by a gold-encrusted frame. The Buddha himself had an LED halo which constantly moved in red, blue, and green lights while fluorescent bulbs harshly lit the green-walled room. I could hear the Burmese chanting, which sounded more like shouting, for an hour at 4:30 A.M. and again at dusk, at the 6:00 P.M. sit. We foreigners simply stumbled through three chants in the evening and were done in fifteen minutes.

The Burmese water trough had four faucets, with a steel cup hanging over each one. Foreigners went to the side of the dining hall, where they could fill their water bottles with water purified by reverse osmosis. I conveniently found an empty water bottle in my room, though I suspected that it was left over from the previous occupant. The idea of washing and sanitizing bottles—or steel cups—has not yet arrived in a country with so few resources.

When we lined up for our one meal of the day at eleven in the morning, we stood in the order of seniority. Monks first, followed by nuns in light pink robes. A handful of Burmese men, a dozen Burmese women, then a handful of foreign men and about ten Western, Chinese, and Malaysian women. This meant I was always last in line.

The Burmese stayed in dorms while we foreigners had our individual rooms. I was happy to see snug-fitting screens on my windows to keep the mosquitoes and other bugs outdoors.

My mattress was an inch thick, like every other mattress I slept on in Burma. The Burmese seem to prefer big, heavy fleece blankets for their nighttime temperatures of 75 degrees. Fortunately, I travel with a pareo, which I use as my sheet.

The abbot of this monastery had several building projects underway, with the names of donors prominently displayed on plaques. One recently constructed conference room proudly displayed the names of several

Malaysian donors, but the top of the list, in the biggest letters, was "Jesus Christ."

I met with Sayadaw U Indaka every day for fifteen minutes to report on my meditation, which his niece translated. My five-day retreat was just long enough to establish a calm mind and to experience one surprising split-second of pure awareness of "knowing," but without perception. Most Westerners who go to Burma to meditate usually stay for a three-month retreat. But it was time to leave, to travel with Connie and go to Laos.

Still, I was happy to go to Burma to meditate, even if only for five days, even if Connie didn't.

Looking for Hua Lor

THE DAY AFTER my meditation retreat ended, Susan, Connie, and I left our friend Myay's condo in Yangon, rode down on the elevator, got into a taxi, and told the driver that we wanted to go to the airport. The taxi pulled out of the parking lot, and Connie asked the cab to pull over. She opened the door, leaned out, and threw up on the street.

Susan and I thought this was just a blip on the screen for Connie-the-world-traveler, who had come to Southeast Asia every winter for more than thirty years to visit her projects in Thailand, Laos, and Burma. However, Connie was still feeling queasy on the airplane from Yangon to Bangkok. Our connecting flight to Vientiane, the capital of Laos, was delayed for five hours due to fog, which meant we would miss our ride to Vang Vieng with our Vermont neighbors, Whit and Tonia, and Tonia's college friend and traveling companion, Missy.

Fortunately, Myanmar Air took pity on Connie and let the three of us into their business-class lounge at the Bangkok airport, where Connie spent the rest of the day reclining in a lounger. Susan and I tried to entice her with free yogurt and hydrating waters and juices, while the two of us were enjoying the free buffet of tropical fruits and Thai snacks.

By the time we flew into Vientiane at 8:00 P.M., Connie was in a wheelchair. Since I'd been to Laos with her before, I knew enough to hurry up and get into line for a Lao visa. The country director of World Education, the NGO that Connie worked for, was there to meet us. He decided to take Connie home with him, and he took Susan and me to a hastily-arranged very nice hotel. Before they left, I gave Connie my stash of Cipro tablets and watched her take one.

The next morning, she was feeling a bit better. Why, oh why, hadn't I forced a Cipro on her earlier? Our plan changed slightly. Susan and I were to be driven to Vang Vieng by a World Education driver, while Connie stayed in Vientiane to recuperate. She sent us on a mission, an adventure of a sort. We were to take a *songtaew*—a tiny Toyota pickup with two wooden plank benches running the length of the bed and facing each other (the word *songthaew* means "two rows")—ten kilometers north of Vang Vieng to a Hmong village. There we were to pay her respects to the village headman, a shaman who had worked for World Education some years earlier. "Go to Phathao and ask for Hua Lor." Easy for her to say. Connie speaks Lao as well as Thai.

After three hours of twisty roads through karst mountains, we arrived at Vang Vieng and met Whit, Tonia, and Missy, who had already scoped out the town. They had taken a morning tour on the Nam Song river in a wooden canoe as long and almost as narrow as a single scull. They had visited the caves in the karst mountain across the river, where villagers had taken refuge from the planes dropping their unused bombs before landing on the air strip in town during the Vietnam War.

The five of us ate lunch on the terrace of a small restaurant decorated with a stockade of bombshells of varying sizes. We admired the bombshells that were sawed in half lengthwise and repurposed as planters overflowing with flowers.

After lunch, we hired a *songthaew* to take the five of us to the village—which wasn't a village at all, at least not as I think of the word *village*. The collection of homes was spread out over a mile in length and maybe half a mile in width over the rolling terrain—each house about a hundred feet from the next and all connected by dirt paths. In fact, we weren't even sure where to disembark from our *songthaew*. The driver suggested one wide spot in the road. We all climbed down from our two rows of seats. We asked for Hua Lor. Nope. Nobody had ever heard of him. We got back into our patient driver's two-rows, and he drove on for another bit, stopping at the village store, which sold very few items and which was obviously not the center of the village. A shaky bridge of four bamboo poles provided a walkway across a twenty-foot-wide ditch.

"We're looking for Hua Lor." Nope. We soldiered on. "Hua Lor?" Another shake of the head. We found a young man who sort of spoke English, and who decided to accompany us on our quest. He was home on a weekend break from his hotel management school. The fifth time we asked, we finally got a response. "Oh, Hua Lor! Why didn't you say so?"

This next young man was a relative of his, and he guided us through a quarter mile of winding paths, past cement-block houses with rusted tin roofs and homes with tatami-mat walls, to the stucco home of Hua Lor. We sat and smiled at each other, met his adult children, and took pictures for about twenty minutes. Then we wound our way back to the main road and our *songtaew*, taking pictures of village life as we went—women doing intricate embroidery, grandmothers resting with children in hammocks, laundry hung on bamboo poles attached to a satellite dish.

Just another daily adventure when you're traveling with, or even without, Connie.

Going. Not Going. Going.

I WAS LOOKING FORWARD to a retreat in the wilderness. Buddha did it. Jesus did it. I've done four vision quests and two self-retreats in the wilds. I love meditating outdoors. My deepest insights have happened in Nature, where the oneness of life is so accessible.

My main motivation for this particular retreat in California was that I wanted to receive teachings from the bhikkhuni, the nun, who was co-teaching the retreat with Susie, the teacher who put this wilderness retreat together. I had last talked to Susie, three years previously, when Bill and I were in Moab, Utah, where she lives. I asked her advice about teaching meditation and relaxed into her wisdom. *Oh,* I felt. *She's not just my classmate Susie. She's deep.*

The teachers. The wild place. Perfect. On Sunday evening, six days prior to departure, my Dharma friend Kim brought me face to face with the facts of my body. My back had been spasming for two weeks, and I couldn't expect that it would like being cooped up in a cross-country airplane seat. Just forty-eight hours earlier, I had been crippled with pain, trying to walk through the one-block street festival on Main Street. Every step hurt.

Really hurt. At 2:30 that day, I had been weeding the garden painlessly. At 3:30, my hip locked into a spasm that didn't let go until the next morning.

"Think of the worst you've felt," said Kim. "Could you walk eight miles in that condition?" *Could I fly across the country in that condition?* I squirmed.

This vision-quest-meets-retreat was an opportunity to live outdoors for two weeks. The off-the-grid (way off the grid) base camp had a large cabin with a few outbuildings, including a kitchen, a sauna, and a hot tub that required a literal fire to be built to heat it up. This private property was one of only six privately owned pieces of land remaining in the King Range National Conservation Area, which stretches along fifty miles of wild California coast. The cabin was located eight miles from the nearest teeny-weeny town, Seal Bay, where the trailhead was.

My friend, Dr. Kim, who also knows Susie, recommended that I not go, because my hip had been spasming ever since I had thrown my back out in my handstand class at the circus school. The sacrum-ilium joint was unhappy, maybe inflamed, and the nearby muscles were compensating. I don't have core strength; I've never had core strength. The problem was, I had been relying on my arm, leg, and back muscles to do what my core should do, and now, as a result of my circus classes, a few of those muscles had rebelled.

Dr. Kim, a podiatrist, was very clear that walking on sand, pebbles, and boulders would demand a lot of core strength, and so, even though I could send my backpack and tent on the little plane that was flying the heavy gear and the food into base camp, I should not even consider the option of walking eight miles, not even with only a minimal daypack.

On Sunday night, I emailed Susie in California. "I'm not coming. I cannot walk the eight miles in, over uneven terrain, not even with just a daypack."

The odd thing was that I didn't feel disappointment that I wasn't going. "Well," I told Bill. "Now I have an extra month at home. Summer in Vermont is beautiful. I don't need to go anywhere. Maybe I'll work on two of my manuscripts."

Bill seemed to be rolling along with this zigzag of plans. My not going to California meant he wouldn't be flying out to meet me. We wouldn't go to Lassen Volcano National Park. We wouldn't go to Crater Lake National Park. We wouldn't see Lake Shasta. We wouldn't see those coastal redwoods. We wouldn't go to the Ashland, Oregon, Shakespeare festival and see a couple of plays.

The next morning, Bill was just starting to agitate with "Well, what are we going to do for our summer vacation, then?" when I checked my email. Susie had replied, "We can fly you in, assuming you're comfortable in a small plane."

Thirty-two years earlier, I was in love with a small-plane pilot in Portland, Oregon. This was one of our early dates—he took me flying. He got me a job with one of his pilot friends who had a flooring company. I called myself a "controller" and did the monthly financial statements and computerized the $2 million-a-year company. It was 1984. Dave, the owner, invited my boyfriend Harlan and me to a fly-in at Lake Shasta. We flew in one of Dave's seaplanes. I had a severe panic attack on the way down to Northern California; I gripped my fingernails into my palms, and silently tried to talk myself down while carrying on a normal conversation with Dave and his wife Jody on headphones over the roar of the engine.

The next morning, several planes went flying up to the top of the Trinity Alps above Lake Shasta. From my perspective, I thought the Piper Cub flying next to us was going to crash into the mountain. Another panic attack. The Cub didn't crash.

We flew home later that day, and that's when I asked Harlan to give me flying lessons. Harlan broke up with me a couple of months later, so I finished out my flying lessons with Dave. I soloed on July 3, 1985, and left Portland the next day to move back to Vermont. That was the end of my piloting small planes.

When Susie, the retreat teacher and wilderness guide, emailed me to ask, "How about if we fly you in on a small plane?" how could I refuse? Of course, I said "yes" to Susie. Sure, put me in the passenger seat for the ten-minute flight to base camp. Even if I have a panic attack, I can be comfortable with uncertainty.

Going. Not going. Going.

You never know what's going to happen. You just never know.

Renting a Car in Arcata

I FORGOT TO TAKE my credit card with me to California. Well, no, that's not quite right. As I was packing, I looked at my credit card, and thought, *No. I'm only going to take my debit card with me.* I have a debit card specifically for traveling. I keep about $1,000 in that account. In case my card is stolen, the most the thieves can get, the most they can charge, is the balance in the account.

I flew to California on a Sunday and arrived in Arcata in Northern California on schedule. I went to the Hertz counter to pick up my reserved car, and the Hertz guy flatly refused to rent me a car without a credit card. "Can I give you my credit card number?" I asked. "No," he said. "We have to run the card through our machine."

The remarkable thing was that I didn't chastise myself for not bringing my credit card. I didn't compare this present moment of not having a credit card to some other imaginary present of having a credit card in my hot little hand. I begged. The Hertz guy stood firm, all 220 pounds of him. He wasn't budging. Meanwhile, the National car rental counter had closed. A few minutes earlier, it had been open. Now, the shutters were drawn, and it was definitely closed. My mind did not compare this present moment to the imaginary moment of if-only-the-National-counter-were-open.

The Arcata airport has two gates—one for departures and one for arrivals. Four flights come in every day from San Francisco, and the same four little airplanes depart every day for SFO. Twenty minutes after my arrival, the United ticket counter was closed. There wasn't even a coffee bar in the airport, only two vending machines. The place was abandoned. I was looking for my two checked bags, along with one other guy looking for his bag. *Yoohoo. Anyone here?* We finally rousted a United employee who had stored our bags while I was wrangling with Mr. Hertz. The airport was too small to have a taxi stand, but I did see a sign: "Airport Shuttle 707-772-1234."

I called. Three minutes later, Russ the shuttle guy called back to say he had found a driver who would pick me up in thirty minutes. The charge for driving the three hours to Seal Bay would be $285. Ouch! But he took my debit card number over the phone. Hey, I would have paid Hertz that much or more, $400 actually, to rent a car for two weeks, only to have it parked in Seal Bay while I was on retreat.

The driver, a local guy named Tom who didn't have anything else to do on a Sunday afternoon, picked me up, and then drove to a mall in Eureka to pick up his girlfriend, who was just getting off work from Victoria's Secret. She was a late-thirties Filipina who had been in this country for a couple of years, thanks to Tom. Tom introduced us. "Just call her Gigi." Gigi chattered on, excited to have this opportunity to see Seal Bay.

"So, Tom," I asked, "how long has it been since you've been to Seal Bay?"

"Oh, about five years," he said as we sped down California Route 1 through a forest of redwoods.

I asked Gigi about her life. She had been a nanny in the United Arab Emirates for six years, starting when she was thirty-two.

"I've heard that foreign workers are abused sometimes," I said.

She nodded.

An hour and forty-five minutes later, we turned off Route 1 to drive through the mountains down to Seal Bay on the coast. I was going to a wilderness retreat on the Lost Coast, and Seal Bay was our departure point. The paved road was European-narrow, not even wide enough to have a white center line, and it was extremely winding. No wonder the builders of California State Route 1—known to most Californians as "Highway 1"—had to leave the coast at Mendocino and continue inland on this section of California's 800-mile long coastal highway until they reached Eureka. Having no Pacific Coast Highway running alongside it is the reason the Lost Coast was "lost." It took strong intention to get to this isolated California coast. Even the locals didn't go there very often. It was way out of the way.

My phone, which had been dotting in and out of service on Highway 1, now simply said *No Service*. No last-minute goodbye phone call to Bill. I had fallen beyond the reach of cyberspace.

Tom covered the twenty-one miles in an hour and dropped me off at the motel where I had made a reservation. I gave him a hefty tip so that he and Gigi could go out to dinner at the only restaurant in Seal Bay—a pizza place.

I quickly met three other people who were also attending the two-week retreat. After twelve hours of sitting in airports, planes, and shuttles, I was happy to take a walk with them toward the beach. The centerpiece of the town was the airstrip where our gear would be departing from the next morning. No little planes were tethered there now, though the strip was surrounded by vacation homes, mostly under 3,000 square feet, whose owners flew in on weekends.

On Monday morning, I called Bill collect from a pay phone. Wow! How long had it been since I had even *seen* a pay phone? And I hadn't made a collect call in, what—twenty years?

Bill chuckled as he answered. I gave him my last-minute instructions. 1) "Bring my credit card with you." 2) "Call the shuttle and tell them I'll call them in two weeks for a ride." I had figured out that no one was driving north toward Arcata; everyone was driving south. But I could probably find a ride out to Highway 1 and have the shuttle pick me up there, wherever "there" on Highway 1 might turn out to be. 3) "When the doctor's office calls with the results of the MRI of my back, call the retreat emergency number if it's metastasized cancer. Otherwise, don't bother." 4) "Goodbye, I love you, and I'll see you when you arrive in Arcata in two weeks."

At 7:30, twenty-seven people, along with the two teachers, convened at the airstrip. The pilot of a little Cessna was one of the co-owners of the private cabin where we would be retreating. He had flown in the cook and the food on Friday. Today, Monday, he would fly in the heavy gear—the tents and sleeping bags and whatever else—so that the retreatants could hike the eight miles to the cabin over the black sand and cobbles. Susie, one of the retreat teachers, had arranged for me and my complaining back to be flown in.

Sam, the pilot, took off with one load of gear. Everyone else drove from the airstrip down to the trailhead on the beach. I remained there alone on the little runway, lounging around on the pile of tents, sleeping bags, and duffel bags. Half an hour later, Sam returned and loaded up his plane again, and then I squeezed into the copilot seat. I enjoyed watching Sam at the controls, and mentally testing myself to see how much I remembered about the dials, the stick, and the nose up while stalling in order to land. Ten minutes later, we were landing on the cinder runway in front of the cabin.

I met Olivia, the cook, and then helped Olivia and Sam get the place ready for company. I cleaned up the two outhouses. I set up my tent and took a two-inch-thick mattress from the cabin, which could probably sleep twenty. Sam, the pilot, was also a surfer. I could easily imagine him and twenty friends sleeping in the rustic, beautiful two-story cabin, which had various nooks for six double-bed mattresses, a pile of two dozen sleeping mats, plus about a dozen sleeping bags, which doubled as comforters.

The kitchen was on the other side of the yard, fully equipped with an industrial stove as well as a wood-burning cookstove, a sink, tile counters, and a large refrigerator. Sam and Olivia realigned the stand-alone solar panels on a pedestal, the source of all the electricity here. As I swept out the bathhouse, I asked Sam about the gravity-fed spring.

An outdoor shower, very attractively done up as the kind of rocky cave you might find on a beach, got its hot water from a wood stove surrounded by a jacket of water. The hot tub, which must be great for chilled-to-the-bone surfers, was a handmade tin tub that could hold five people.

After lunch, Sam departed for Eureka. I watched the wildlife. I surprised a deer in the side yard where my tent rested in what I called the hummingbird garden. A dozen hummingbirds of three or four different types were dashing about claiming this or that flowering shrub as their territory. I watched a bunny fall asleep on the black sand.

At about four o'clock, I walked to the edge of Sandy Flat to await the arrival of my fellow retreatants. Sandy Flat is a mile and a half long and a third of a mile wide. The mile-long cinder runway was a logging road before the Bureau of Land Management bought up most of the Lost Coast in the 1970s to create the King Range National Conservation Area for public recreation. Forty years later, only six pieces of private property remain in this 150-square-mile wilderness.

Soon, I saw a line of thirty people walking toward me. They clambered up the rocks onto Sandy Flat, and began walking down the trail through the tall brown grass. I waited until the end, silently greeted each person as they passed, and then joined the line myself.

The retreat had officially begun.

My concentration at the beginning of the retreat was surprisingly good, despite those two little worries, which buzzed through my mind like hummingbirds trying to claim territory, but then disappeared for a while as I told myself, *I don't need to know how I'm getting back to Arcata; that's twelve days from now.* Or: *If the MRI was bad news, Bill would have called the emergency number. No news is good news.* Since I hadn't heard anything by Thursday, the fourth day, I could really settle down and just forget about the results of the MRI altogether.

The retreat was very good. Sitting, meditating outdoors for two weeks—well, you can't beat that. Meditating under a tree, with a person in ocher robes sitting at the base of the tree, seems to be just the way it should be. My back barely complained. I told Susie, the teacher and wilderness guide, that I expected to be able to walk out, especially since I could send all my gear on the airplane.

On the last evening of our fourteen-day retreat, Susie told me that she had arranged for Sam-the-pilot to fly me back to Eureka. Wow! That would be easy, fast, and fun too. So, I walked the eight miles out with everyone else, then got into Sam's Cessna and flew to a private airfield in Eureka. Susie had told me I would need to call a cab, and I prepared to do so.

"Where am I right now?" I asked Sam.

"Murray Field," he said. "Where are you going?"

"The Holiday Inn Express near the Arcata airport. My husband's flying in tonight at midnight."

"Oh, that's on my way," he said. "I'll drop you off."

I checked into the Holiday Inn Express and called Bill. Who was still in Hartford. "My flight was canceled," he said. "I'm flying out at six in the morning."

Oh, sigh. After I hung up, I walked the quarter mile to the airport, finding some deliciously ripe blackberries on the way—big and juicy. I talked to the National car rental guy. "We don't have any cars," he said. "And we can't rent to you without a credit card."

Okay, so what was I going to do on Monday? I could feel the thought of *a wasted day of vacation* knocking on the door of my mind, but I didn't open that door. Hmm.

The Holiday Inn Express cost $169 a night and was located in a pasture. I looked on Trip Advisor and saw that the closest restaurant was 2.5 miles away. I could probably walk there before dark, but I had already walked eight miles that day, and I could feel my back stiffening up. The hotel shuttle was not allowed to take me to a restaurant, but luckily Round Table Pizza would deliver to my room.

The next morning, I checked out of my room, leaving my luggage—my roller bag and a monster roller bag containing my camping gear—in a closet at the Holiday Inn. I begged the shuttle driver to take me to McKinleyville, three miles away, but he said he could not. He did, however, drive me about a third of a mile beyond his route and dropped me off on Central Avenue. My plan was to go spend the day at the library and catch up on two weeks' worth of email.

I began walking with my daypack on my back. An hour later, I arrived at the library, which, I discovered, was closed on Mondays. I sat outside on a bench, catching the library's wi-fi, for about twenty minutes. I chatted with a lady who was returning a Lonely Planet book on Iceland. "I love Iceland," I said.

"We're flying there tomorrow," she replied.

I looked across the parking lot to Azalea Hall, home of the McKinleyville Senior Center. *Go on, Cheryl,* I told myself. *But I'm not a senior-center-type person,* I replied to myself, and then countered, *Well, today you are. You have white hair. You are old enough to walk in there.* So, I took a deep breath and walked into the bare-bones Senior Center—a large room with three long tables on one side and two long tables on the other. A Latino man was busily arranging muffins and other bread products on a shelf. A man was on a computer at the far end of the room. He left after about half an hour, and I spent the next three hours weeding out my email. Bill called me from Chicago O'Hare and then from SFO. Florence, a wrinkled lady in a fantastic blond wig, started telling me about growing up in the area, about a recent funeral and a recent wedding. She recommended the small tourist town of Trinidad to me, so I looked it up on Trip Advisor and made a reservation at the Sea Cliff View Motel for that night.

The senior center closed at four, and Bill wouldn't arrive until seven, so I wandered around. I found a thrift store and bought fleece pullovers for the windy, and therefore chilly, California coast. I went to Safeway and bought a snack of watermelon chunks. Trip Advisor alerted me that I was close to McKinleyville's only tourist attraction—the tallest totem pole in the world—and there it was, right next to Safeway. Who says you can't be a tourist on foot?

I couldn't resist a store called Funk Shui and bought a hula hoop, which I thought would be good for exercising my back. I walked the three miles back to the little airport, carrying the hula hoop, and sat in the lounge with half a dozen other people. The lady next to me told me her very interesting life story.

Bill was nearly the last one off his plane. We got in line at the Hertz counter. Bill gave me my credit card, which he had brought with him, and I plunked it down and said to Jacob-the-bear behind the counter, "Now I'm ready to pick up our car."

He said, "Since your reservation was for this morning and you didn't show up, your reservation was canceled after two hours. We don't have any cars, and we won't have any cars until day after tomorrow." The force of his words nearly pushed me backward into Bill. I glanced over at the National counter, which had been open ten minutes ago, but was now closed.

"Cheryl," Bill growled. "Why didn't you change the reservation?"

I honestly had not even considered the possibility of cancellation.

The man in a suit behind us in line said, "I can give you a ride."

Bill said, "Let's stay at the Holiday Inn." No way did I want to spend another $169 and order another $30 pizza for dinner, not even my favorite with anchovies and olives.

"I'll call Enterprise tomorrow," I said. "They don't open until 9:00." I knew this from recent experience, since I had called them at 8:00 that morning trying to beg a car from them, but had to leave a message.

The man in a suit behind us, an Indian-American, said, "Enterprise will pick you up."

That clinched my decision. "Thanks for your offer," I said. "We're going ten miles north. Are you sure you don't mind?"

"I'm going to a medical conference in Eureka tomorrow," he said.

"But Eureka is twelve miles south of here," I said.

"Oh, I don't mind," he said. "I hate being stranded myself."

We followed him out to his blue Chevy Spark, which had enough room in the trunk for our Good Samaritan's roller bag and Bill's daypack. We put Bill's roller bag next to me on the back seat, along with my daypack and hula hoop. Then we stopped at the Holiday Inn Express to pick up my roller bag. The giant bag of camping gear would have to spend the night in the Holiday Inn's closet by itself.

Siri gave us directions to the Sea Cliff View motel in Trinidad. We cruised on to Highway 1, and soon we were driving alongside the ocean.

"I lived in New York when I first came to this country," our driver, named Chuck, said. "But when I moved to California, I spent every weekend just driving along the coast for about a year, until I finally got tired of it."

Within minutes we found the motel, and Chuck departed in his miniature rental car.

Our host, Bob, showed us to our room. We asked about where to have dinner. He began to tell us about the town of Trinidad, three miles to the south.

Oops. "Well, as you see," I said, "we don't have a car, so..."

"The best restaurant in town is just a hundred yards down the road," Bob said. "Larrupin. Do you know that word?"

Bill and I shook our heads. "Never heard of it."

"Well, here in the West, we say the food is larrupin' good. And the food there is really, really good."

So, Bill and I walked down the road to the Larrupin Restaurant and had a fine meal. We walked back in the dark, because we had forgotten to bring flashlights. By this time, it was past midnight in Bill's East Coast time, and he was aching to lie down and stretch out. Within seconds of returning to our motel room, he was snoozing. I quickly fell asleep, too, happy to have Bill next to me, but I woke up at 2:00 A.M., when night mind kicked in and reviewed all the unknowns, over and over. *Where to get a car? Where to get a car?* After an hour, it occurred to me that even if there were no rental cars in Arcata or Eureka, I could buy a used car now that I had my credit card. We were going to continue this vacation, by hook or by crook. I finally fell asleep, just before dawn.

Bob, a former LAPD detective, had told us that the best coffee in town was at the Beachcomber Cafe. "And the characters that hang out there," he said, "still think it's 1962. You should hear their stories."

He said he'd drive us down there at nine in the morning, but at 9:00 A.M. I was calling Enterprise, who said they'd come and pick us up (*Bless you, Chuck*). I asked Bob for his recommendation of where to spend our second night in Trinidad, and he suggested the Emerald Forest, so I called them for a cabin.

We dropped our suitcases at the Emerald Forest on our way into town. "Town" turned out to be one block long, much smaller than I imagined. We ordered breakfast. Bob got his Mason jar of coffee and bade us goodbye. Ten minutes later, a white car with beads of water on the back window pulled up in front of the cafe, and I went out to greet the Enterprise driver, who introduced himself as Steve. Bill was still waiting for our slow order, and Steve said he'd wait.

Steve was thin, and he was probably on the spectrum; he was a bit odd, and he followed the traffic rules to a T. He drove us into Arcata and told us that the food co-op was just three blocks from the Enterprise office. We could stock up on travel snacks there.

Before we drove away in our sparkling white Kia, I hugged Joe the Enterprise manager and Steve the driver. After two weeks and two days of wanting a rental car, I was finally behind the wheel, thanks to the generosity of total strangers—Sam the pilot, Chuck with the tiny blue rental car, Bob the motel owner, the friendly folks at the McKinleyville senior center, and Steve, the Enterprise driver. Life just kept unfolding, offering one helping hand after another, and carrying me along in ways I never could have imagined, even without a credit card.

The Postage Stamp Tour

I F   Y O U   H A V E only one day to spend in Norway, you
can take the Norway-in-a-Nutshell tour. From Oslo,
take the train toward Bergen. At the highest point of
ice and snow, in Myrdal, change for a short, local train
that daringly descends alongside a cascade of a river.
The train makes one stop on a bridge where you can
take pictures of the spectacular scenery—deep green
valleys surrounded by snow-capped mountains, even in
mid-summer.

A few more kilometers, and you arrive at the town
of Flåm (pronounced "phlegm") at the head of the
Aurlandsfjord. Hop on a ferry down the fjord that
turns left into the next fjord, Nærøyfjord. Disembark in
the town of Gudvangen and get on a bus, which takes
you up thirteen hairpin turns, full of thrilling vistas,
and then becomes even more thrilling—and terrify-
ing—when your uphill bus meets a downhill bus on the
one-and-a-half-lane road and has to back down to the
hairpin turn.

By the end of the day, you're back in Oslo and ready
to fly on to the next country on your one-week tour of
Scandinavia.

While I was on a meditation retreat in England, I took what I called the Postage Stamp tour. I was limited, but not by time, for I had an entire month-long silent retreat in the low, rolling hills of Devon. Rather, I was limited by how far I could walk in the hour and a half after lunch. A five-mile round trip meant I could go no farther away than two and a half miles.

Yet, within a two-mile radius—my postage stamp—I had an entire tour of England. My guide was a laminated map of local roads, about the size of a recipe card.

Let me begin chronologically, in terms of British history as I discovered it in the backyard of the retreat center.

Tramping off through the sheep pastures, as many of these expeditions began, cutting around the edge of the nearby village, Denbury, and walking up a brushy lane between fields to a high point of land brought me to that intriguing spot marked on my little 3" x 5" map as "Tumuli." This out-of-the-way wooded site was a 4,500-year-old hill fort. And, as a surprisingly placed plaque told me, it was also the home of a people called Devons. Hence, the local town—borough of the Devons—De(vo)nbury.

Another plaque identified the 3,000-year-old mound inside this hill fort as the grave of a chieftain of the Devon people. Really, this was quite a satisfying discovery after I had just washed the luncheon dishes of forty people.

I was practicing a 2,600-year-old tradition. While

the Buddha walked the earth in northern India, the native peoples of Devon were hunting and gathering right here.

Around 450 CE, this 500-foot-tall hill was the last holdout of the Angles before they were finally overrun by the Saxons. At about the same time in Sri Lanka, Buddhaghosa was editing the *Visuddhimagga* (*The Path of Purification*), the condensed and systematized teachings of the Buddha.

Another day, while walking along a one-lane paved road, I saw that two cars were going to pass each other approximately right where I was located. I quickly stepped into the eight-foot-tall hedgerow, and found myself standing in the bottom of a disused well. A tall wall rose up beside me, all inside the hedgerow. The hedges in Devon date from 800 to 1500 CE.

Another day, on another road, I found a nameless fortification from the Middle Ages.

The Denbury church in town was founded by Aeldred, who crowned William the Conqueror in 1066.

The thirteenth-century parish church next to the retreat center was closed up, but several of my walks began with strolling through the church graveyard, where I concocted stories from the names, dates, and epitaphs on the tombstones.

Mary MacNamara died in 1844, aged fifty. Apparently from Ireland, she devoted her life to the children who lived in the nearby manor house and was so much beloved by them that she was honored with a gravestone.

The garden of the retreat center was bounded by high walls on two sides. From the road, I could see that these twenty-foot-high walls were the remains of an abbey. The abbeys were dissolved in 1539 by Henry VIII, and their stones used for new construction, which brings me to the retreat center itself.

Open the four-foot-wide front door, and you find yourself walking on flagstones worn smooth by 450 years of feet walking back and forth. The retreat center is a former convent, which was a former manor house, built in 1588 by prisoners of war from the Spanish Armada. The kernel of that manor house is the exceedingly drafty hallway, kitchen, and a retrofit Victorian bathroom, complete with pull chain from the tank above your head, circa 1900.

The manor house was added onto in 1790, and these roomier rooms remind me of the game of Clue—library, lounge, dining room, drawing room, conservatory. We meditators were all silently seeking the clues that would help us notice the death of the ego and perhaps experience a moment of the deathless.

In 1925, the rambling manor house became a Diocesan retreat center, but that did not flourish. In 1939, this house and grounds were given to the Sisters of St. Gabriel, who ran it as a shelter for children from London to protect them from the bombing. (Never mind that there was a firing range in nearby Denbury.)

The manor-house-cum-convent had an additional dormitory wing built on in 1954, perhaps because of the shortage of men to marry in the postwar years; the dormitory was added in 1960. Another wing was added in 1966. Then the sexual revolution began, Pope Paul approved the reforms known as Vatican II, and the numbers of sisters declined.

Gaia House bought the property in 1996, and the former convent can now house sixty retreatants, plus a staff of twelve.

After sitting for forty-five minutes in the drafty meditation hall (the former chapel, built in 1955), I would walk up to the top of the back garden and sit on a bench in a three-sided little garden house and gaze out over the rolling green pastures. In the distance, I could just see the Dartmoor, and the 1,500-foot-tall stack of granite rock called Hay Tor.

Two weeks into my stay, I was silently sitting, gazing, when a tall man walked past me and continued on behind the garden house to the very top of the garden. *Prince Charles! No!*

By this time, I recognized all the coats and hats of my co-retreatants, even if I didn't know their names. The red windbreaker and hand-knit brown woolen hat were strangers to me. A minute later, the man walked past me, heading downhill. He still looked like Prince Charles.

What do you do when you're in the middle of a month of silence and you want to shout, *Hey! Is that really Prince Charles?* Even though I was dying to say something, there was no one I could say it to.

I walked slowly and silently down the small hill back

to the meditation hall and noted two men leaning on a fence, talking to each other. People talking on a silent retreat? Very strange. Were they bodyguards?

Since a common British postage stamp shows the head of Queen Elizabeth, the mother of Prince Charles, that sighting of royalty put the official stamp on my Postage Stamp Tour of England that November.

While my meditating self was on retreat, my inner historian delighted in tramping through the nearby sheep pastures and trekking on the nearby roads reading the silent shards of British history.

BURTON
ISLAND

Rainy Morning
at Burton Island

I WOKE UP TO the sound of a few raindrops spattering on my tent. I reached for my iPhone and pushed the Weather app. Clouds all day, with the sun peeking out at ten and eleven. Lightning bolts all afternoon.

Maybe I should pack up and leave the lake a day early? I have so much to do at home. It's August 1, and I'm going to be home only five days this month. Wouldn't one more day be a bonus? What's really getting me down is the thought of packing my roller bag ten days from now for five vacations in a row—opera, camping, retreat, Oregon, and Idaho. Leave home August 13 and return September 14.

Vacation = stress. How can that be? I pack up the solar collector that charges my iPhone, but then decide to stick it out at the state park for the day, despite the clouds. I can meditate in the lean-to all day before going to a day-long retreat in central Vermont tomorrow.

As soon as I put on my rain jacket and walk to the bathroom, the sprinkles stop. On the other side of the lake, I can see blue sky. I shed my raincoat and take my meditation cushion to the beach. I'm in fleece pants and a light merino wool sweater, ready for the cloudy breezes.

Ten minutes into meditation, I feel the morning sun streaming onto me. After meditation, I return to my campsite, change into shorts and a tank top, and take my bowl of granola down to the beach. While I'm talking to Bill on my phone, I see that it has less than 20 percent left on the battery, despite my keeping it in airplane mode most of the day. I return my dirty bowl to my campsite and pick up my iPad-sized solar collector to charge my iPhone.

The lake ripples. I read an inspirational book, and the thought crosses my mind, *If I died tomorrow, I would not regret this beautiful blue-sky morning at the lake, doing nothing.* Home calls like a Siren—so many things to do. My self wants to run away from a peaceful day and get busy doing, doing something, doing anything.

Beach, lapping water, distant winds. Sunshine recharging my iPhone battery. And mine.

Meditation on the Lake

T HE GRAY-BLUE SKY hints at pink as I unzip my tent door. Crawling out onto dew-damp grass, I slide into plastic sandals, then reach back into the tent for a short Thermarest pad that buckles itself into a seat. Into this turquoise nylon square clamshell, I stuff a folded beach towel, a Dharma book, a clock, and a meditation shawl.

I walk toward a shrubby border of sumac, white cedars, and young elms. The path opens onto a beach of flat black slate rocks, small and still sharp at their corners.

I put down my turquoise clamshell near the lake and turn to the kayaks. I push the blue one into the water and hop in, pushing out from shore. After a few paddle strokes, I rest the paddle in front of me.

Facing east, I drift on glassy water and watch the pink dawn spread over distant mountains. This morning, I notice I am floating over a mussel nursery bed, with shells as big as my knuckles clinging to mossy underwater rocks.

After a while, I paddle back to shore and beach the kayak. I settle on top of my Thermarest, unbuckling it so that I can sit on my folded beach towel and rest my ankles on the pad. I read two pages of the Dharma book before I hear footsteps crunching rocks behind me.

Here comes Connie, my neighbor with whom I meditate most mornings at home. More footsteps, this time her brother, David, another neighbor who learned to meditate at a Zen center at college. He only sits with us when I go to Connie's house for meditation on Saturday mornings. His wife Susan joins us. My next-door neighbor Diana arrives with her own short Thermarest. Due to a bad back, she meditates lying down.

Diana usually brings an inspirational passage, and she reads a paragraph from a Dharma book now. Connie leads the chant of the Loving-Kindness Sutta. I set the timer, and we settle into twenty-five minutes of wave-lapping bird-chirping stillness.

It's a beautiful beginning to every day during this week of camping at the lake with my neighbors.

Burton Island Sunset

AFTER DINNER AT the picnic table at six o'clock, people start wandering down to the beach, each with a book in one hand and a folding lawn chair in the other. The sun is still well above the horizon by the time the two after-dinner dishwashers arrive at around seven.

Nowadays, we are only eight adults with reading glasses, and one thirty-one-year-old man with a developmental delay. But not so long ago, our tribe had fourteen or sixteen adults with an equal number of children.

Jane and Whit are reading thick historical or political books. Tonia and Connie are reading novels that are on the *New York Times* best-seller list. Diana and John are reading books from the *NYT* best-selling nonfiction list. David is reading a murder mystery. Cheryl is doing sudoku. Nathan is saying, "I want a fire. I want a fire." He does love a good campfire.

Every once in a while, conversation breaks out, and people glance up to notice the clouds and predict the sunset.

"It'll be a good one tonight."

"I don't think we'll have a sunset tonight."

"Do you think we'll see a green flash?"

This last question was the question Rich asked every year, and he died in 2004. Some of his ashes are scattered here on this little island that is a Vermont State Park.

Half an hour before sunset, two or four people take to kayaks and paddle out on the dark-blue lake, which is rich with golden coins of the sun's reflection. A few hundred feet out from shore, the kayakers rest their paddles, allowing themselves to drift toward the sunset that is now turning the clouds golden.

On shore, the light grows dim as the sun hides behind a thin cloud and then peeks out again. People set down their books on the slaty beach. Now we're all paying attention to the sunset.

We are neighbors; where we live in the heavily forested Vermont hills, we can see neither sunset nor sunrise. Here, we attend closely to the details of the sun resting on the horizon, and sinking, sinking from view.

The kayakers return and stow the kayaks, upside down and out of reach of the lake.

Just after sunset, two dozen seagulls fly from east to west. We joke that they've spent the day at the St. Albans landfill, and now they're going home to one of the little islands five or six miles west of here. Cedar waxwings dart out of nearby trees to catch mosquitoes.

On a cloudy day, when the sunset is mostly gray, people disperse to their tents, but ordinarily we observe the cloud details of the 8:23 P.M. sunset until all the golden-cherry-orange-green color has leaked out of the sky. The heavens turn Maxfield Parrish blue, a bright star begins to twinkle, and we are satisfied with this summer day of living outdoors with Nature.

One by one, or two by two, people fold their chairs and head to the campground bathroom, disappearing into the darkness with flashlights in hand but not turned on.

And now to sleep, listening to the lake sloshing on the shore and a chorus of crickets chirping outside our tents.

Phones at Burton Island State Park

Back in the 1990s, I had to walk seven minutes to the pay phone at the camp store, down by the marina, in order to call Bill at home, using my phone card. In 1998, David brought his cell phone to Burton Island, but had to keep it out of sight because it irritated the rest of us. In 2000 Whit had a Nokia phone, and the following year he received a phone call from Ireland and a conference call from Italy.

In 2004, I joined the twenty-first century and got rid of the bag phone I'd been carrying in my car since 1992 in favor of a flip phone. About half of us had flip phones, but they were still unwelcome at our campsite, with one exception.

Reservations for our next year's July vacation on Burton Island had to be made on August 1. In 2004, at 9:00 A.M. sharp, seven of us sat around the picnic table on our cell phones dialing and redialing the phone number for the Vermont Department of Parks. Finally, Michael, that charmer, got through.

By 2010, AT&T had bought out my carrier, Unicel,

so I was the first in my neighborhood to convert to an iPhone and pay $78 a month for the privilege, instead of the $51 a month I had paid to Unicel. Most of my neighbors switched to Verizon, which provided better coverage in our hill-and-narrow-valley area of southeastern Vermont.

Now came the question of charging the iPhone, whose batteries didn't last four days, as the flip phone batteries did. I plugged my iPhone into the only available electric outlet—the socket on the light fixture over the mirror in the women's bathroom—and left it there for three hours. One slight problem was that when the bathroom lights were turned off, as they would be during daylight hours, the charge to the phone was also turned off. It took a bit of double-checking in the middle of the day to make sure the lights were still on.

In 2013 I upgraded from an iPhone 3G to a 4G, and by this time the smart-phone users at our campsite outnumbered the troglodytes who were using TrackFones. Now phone conversations from lawn chairs were a common occurrence, not irritating anyone. People texted, sometimes with mutual friends, updating the rest of us on the details of life at home.

A Kindle app on an iPhone is a lot lighter to carry than a bag of books, and easier for aging eyes to read when you're lying in your tent at nine o'clock at night.

I invested in a solar collector, about the size of an iPad, so that one or two people could charge their phones or iPods from the sun each day. So now our phones are as close as our pockets. Instead of dimes or quarters for the pay phone, all we need is the sun. Of course, now *I* am supplying the phone instead of AT&T. And now I am paying them $95 a month for phone service.

When you're camping on an island, you don't need a watch, and you don't really need a phone. It takes fortitude to decide to limit your communication, especially when you're carrying it around in your pocket.

Lack of instant communication gives rise to calm. After a while, almost imperceptibly, calm gives rise to joy. When you're camping on an island, joy and calm are all around you—as you watch the sunrise on the still lake, as you see a dragonfly breathe while you paddle your kayak, or as you watch seven ducklings trail a mother duck. Happiness is at your fingertips as long as you keep your fingertips off your smart phone and the virtual reality that distracts you from the vivid reality of sights, sounds, smells, touches, and tastes surrounding you in this very life in HD. Touch your life instead of a screen, and taste, really taste, your one-and-only life.

ELEMENTS:
Earth, Water, Air, & Fire

Meat to Meat

NATIVE AMERICANS AND other hunter societies saw directly that the meat they were eating put meat on their own bones. Sometimes they ate the heart or liver of a strong buffalo or bear so that they themselves would have a strong heart or liver. Nowadays, we find that belief to be quaint or perhaps distasteful, but I think they were seeing something we have lost sight of.

I take a bite of chicken or salmon. That meat, which is so obviously not me, becomes transmuted into my skin and bones, my flesh, and my blood. Who's to say exactly where the bite of chicken goes in my body, but some of it does become my own flesh, my own muscle.

When did that not-me (chicken) become "me"? When did it become "my" flesh? "My" body? Is it really "mine"?

Let me express gratitude to that cod or that turkey. The meat on my bones is not really so different from the meat I'm masticating. I borrow their flesh to nourish my own flesh. They are lending me their muscle so that I can have some muscle of "my own."

Sister chicken. Brother beef. Sister salmon. Brother bison.

The Earth Element of Calcium

Bones, as we know, are made of calcium and phosphorus, with trace amounts of carbon, potassium, sodium, and magnesium.

In Buddhist meditation, we contemplate the ancient chemistry of earth, water, air, and fire. We could say, as we learned in eighth-grade science, that solids (earth), liquids (water), gases (air), and heat (fire) are required to transmute one substance to another. We say that bones are hard, and thus they represent the earth element.

Women past menopause take a handful of "earth elements" every day when we swallow our calcium-magnesium pills.

Where does calcium come from? Health supplement entrepreneurs take it from various things: calcium carbonate comes from shells and coral reefs. I've settled on the naturopath's recommendation of calcium citrate, which is an insoluble precipitate in the production of citric acid. In other words, calcium comes from some form of limestone in the earth.

In meditation, we focus on the hard bits of the body: bones, teeth, fingernails, and toenails, and we call it "earth." If we could notice kidney stones, gallstones, or salivary duct stones, we could include these stones also as representatives of the earth element.

Then we notice that the earth element is outside us *and* inside us. Once it comes inside us, it's still the same as it was outside. Only now, we have the habit of calling it "me" and "mine." Ladies, take a close look at those calcium pills you are swallowing. You buy them at the store, and you're sure that you are you, and pills are pills. Then you shake one or five into your hand, and you're still sure that you are you and pills are pills. You swallow them, and then what? They are no longer pills. Suddenly they are you. That calcium becomes "your" bones, "your" teeth, "your" nails.

You have to agree that's a real magic trick. It's "you" today, yet if we cremated your body tomorrow, it would be ashes to ashes, dust to dust, earth back to earth.

Ha! It never is mine in the first place. Calcium begins as calcium, enters as calcium, and leaves as calcium. There's no "me" or "mine." Just an impersonal coagulation of elements. The earth element always is simply on loan to me, just passing through.

Aging Bones

HER AGING BODY creaks and groans like a house at night in a strong wind. The edifice is still strong, still able to withstand the whims of nature, but not as lithe and shiny new as it once was.

Her back squeaks and pings. She lubricates it every night with a capsule of fish oil, every morning with a tablet of glucosamine from the exoskeletons of crustaceans and chondroitin from shark cartilage, chicken gristle, and pigs' ears. The formula keeps the aches at bay. She doesn't notice the good they're doing until she forgets to take the glucosamine-chondroitin for a few days in a row. Then the ping begins again, like a car engine running on low octane.

She eats an even better diet now, not so tempted by the cravings of the past. Kale to lower cholesterol, and the other green leaves she has been slow to friendly up to. Less sugar, and an apple, if not every day, then at least every week. She carries one in the car, so she won't be tempted to stop at a mini-mart with its sweet and salty offerings.

Maybe her digestion is like that of an elephant, which is so inefficient that elephant poop looks like little round bales of hay. The green has been extracted; the fiber dried by metabolism, but the inner composting is of small nutritional value. No wonder elephants have to eat such volumes. No wonder they need six sets of teeth.

Her own teeth are aging, too. By her mid-sixties, she calculates she's spent $400 per tooth just to keep them all in her head. A few of those teeth cost two or three thousand dollars apiece, what with root canal, crown, fillings, and gum surgery. She wonders what will happen to her gold fillings when her body is cremated at the end. She's seen men from the lowest caste in India sweep cremains into the Ganges, first sifting through them with their fingers in search of just such gold nuggets.

Gold and silver in the teeth, which are themselves made of calcium and phosphorous. As are her bones. Really, can they even be called "her" bones? Calcium is just traveling through her body, any body. Calcium from milk, from the hard water she drinks two quarts of every day. Calcium from those green leaves she's finally deigned to like. Calcium from the lime she throws on the vegetable garden, which grows up through plants and then passes into her body, and then out again. Is that "her" calcium"? Are those really "her" bones? Or is it just stardust recirculating, recycling itself into oh-so-many different life forms? A sort of magic trick: "What form shall I take this time?" A bone, a tooth, a leaf of kale.

Her aging body creaks and groans as the calcium leaches out, milligram by milligram, returning in one form or another to the earth from which it came.

The Aging Water Heater

O UR HOT WATER is lukewarm, and I don't like to take a shower in tepid water.

Our water heater has coils inside, and those coils are caked with calcium. The water from our well is hard. Hard water. An odd combination of words when you stop to think about is. Water is soft, flowing. How can it be "hard"?

But we know what that means. Some hard element is invisibly dissolved in the water. Here in Vermont, it's calcium. Where I grew up in Indiana, it was iron—rusty spots grew around the toilet bowl or under the steady drip of the bathtub faucet.

Every month or two, when I pour hot water over my teabag, a flake or two of white calcium shakes itself out of the tea kettle. If I open the tea kettle lid, I can see that the inside is caked with a thin rime of white calcium. I scrub it out, and the tea kettle is clean as a whistle for the next bath of hot water.

I can't scrub out the water heater, nor can I see inside it. In 1980, I was told that the life of the water heater was thirty years, so for the past five years, I've been awaiting the inevitable: the heating coils are calcified.

The calcification must be so thick that heat no longer transfers from the coils to the water. Maybe the bottom of the water heater is one solid block of lime turned to stone?

We women are actually quite familiar with this process of calcification. Calcium leaches out of our bones. Early in menopause we call it osteopenia. The inevitable is coming, and its name is osteoporosis. Where does the calcium go?

I recently read *Being Mortal*, by Boston surgeon Atul Gawande. He tells of reaching into an old lady's belly and feeling the coils of intestines to be slightly crunchy. Calcium leaches onto other organs and into various tissues as well. My saliva has a high calcium content, which translates into a thick layer of plaque on my teeth. A certain type of breast cancer is called calcifications.

The element of calcium is on the move—in the body and in my water heater. The water heater can be replaced. The body... well, although there are many replacement parts, including bone joints such as hips, knees, and shoulders, our bones themselves are not replaceable. We await the inevitable. The body, our body, reaches its life expectancy and begins to cool down and become tepid.

The calcium of life and the water of life are no longer in perfect balance, and the life energy fades.

Goodbye, dear water heater.

Air Full of Water

THE AIR IS full of water in the early mornings of September. I wake up in a cloud. Lake Sunapee below has dissolved into air and now rises and spreads, filling all the low ground with misty air. I can see as well as feel 100 percent humidity. This morning, I breathe a rich mixture of water-air.

The body of earth, the ground with its green grass-hair cover, is soaking wet as the thick gray fog begins to lighten up with sunrise colors of golden peach pink. I walk through this mist, this earth-bound cloud, leaving my trail in the wet grass. An uncertain trail, not knowing where it is going. Going nowhere in particular, in fact. Simply being.

Water—shall we say the risen lake?—permeates everything this sunrising morning—the air, the grass, the ground. My bare feet are soaking wet, as is the rainfly on my tent.

In a cloud, the line between heaven and earth is indistinct or even invisible. Where does one end and the other begin? A shadow emerges through the mist. Only by habit and expectation do I call it "a person" as this darker mist approaches. When she joins our silent circle of early risers, I finally recognize her particularity.

Soon, the sun burns this mist into thin air. In the distance, I see a cloud bank rising over the wooded landscape. The sun shines everything into distinctness, and I am I and you are you again. My mind relaxes into these recognizable categories, for I am a lover of words and the categories that those words convey.

But really, really, you are mist, and I am mist, moving over the earth, trackless as a stick drawing a line in water. Soon enough, my footprints are washed from the beach; my tracks in the wet grass are dried to invisibility.

What is real is invisible to our eyes, which search for hard outlines, which seek distinctness, which want to discriminate one thing from another.

In this moment of sunrise, we can see that we ourselves are just a mist of water molecules—a conscious blob of protoplasm that transmits seeing, hearing, and feeling. As the sun rises on our upturned faces, you become you and I become I, and for these next twelve hours of daylight, we believe that we are separate. After sunset, the slim weight of the night's new moon does not entice us into the indistinctness of darkness, where we are once again one with all, which is all we ever are.

Water in Thin Air

THE SUMMER THAT Bill wore a leg brace, after he had knee surgery for a severed quadriceps tendon, he asked me to empty the dehumidifier in his music studio every two or three days. It seems a miracle that plain, clear air can produce a gallon of water a day from a single room.

Bill, the musician, is very particular about his baby grand piano. He babies it by maintaining 55 percent humidity in his studio all year. This means humidifying in the winter—adding a gallon of water a day—and dehumidifying in the summer.

Sound is one of the first things Bill notices in a new place. He tests the sound by clapping his hands to hear the resonance in a room, an auditorium, or an outdoor amphitheater. He didn't want soundproofing on the ceiling, because it would deaden the sound. So, we settled on parasols hanging upside down in his basement studio; parasols hide all the water pipes and electric wires running in their orderly fashion alongside the joists, yet they maintain Bill's acoustical balance.

Five feet away from the humidifier/dehumidifier sit the washer and dryer. The washer adds water to clothes, and the dryer subtracts it. In the winter, we usually use a drying rack and thus the wet clothes add humidity to Bill's music studio. Where does the wetness of the laundered clothes go? Into the air, where it becomes invisible but felt as humidity on his skin.

In the summer, the dehumidifier wrings water out of the air, changing water from its humid gaseous state into its liquid form. Converting water to steam by boiling water seems so ordinary. Yet converting a steamy climate to a dry one, with water separated out by means of a dehumidifier, seems a marvel.

Upstairs, summer hangs heavy, hot, and sweltering. Open the door to the daylight basement where Bill's studio is, and you descend into his man-cave—cool and dry. The basement is naturally twenty degrees cooler than the house. Thanks to the dehumidifier, the air is dry and somehow easier to breathe. I feel I could float in this light cool air for the rest of the day. I sit in his recliner and push back, relaxing as I look at the parasols covering the ceiling.

Water is hiding in thin air, and I don't even notice. It's as invisible as sound.

Where Am I From?

I~N~ J~UNE~ 2016, I did a wilderness retreat on the Lost Coast of California for two weeks. The Pacific Ocean surfed onto a black sand beach about 400 feet away, roaring in my ears day and night, sounding as if I were camping between two runways with a jet taking off every ten seconds.

I lived in a tent, and I meditated outdoors, 24/7. I lived out in the elements, as they say—subject to wind, rain, heat, and cold—day and night. The retreat was a great opportunity to contemplate the elements of earth, water, fire, air.

Water came from a gravity-fed spring into two faucets in the yard. Every morning, I stood and brushed my teeth at one of the faucets, looking up at the burned trees on the forest-fired mountain, where the water came from a spring about 200 feet above us. At the back of the property, where the broad, sandy flat met the mountain, an outdoor shower had been constructed of beach boulders cemented together. The water for the shower was heated by a wood stove. My yogi job was building the driftwood fire in the wood stove every evening after dinner, to heat up the water circulating in the metal jacket surrounding the wood stove, which then flowed directly to the shower.

The cold spring water also flowed via a faucet into a hot tub, and it was someone's job to start the driftwood fire every afternoon to heat up the tub, which was half-full of water. At 8:00 P.M., the first person to the hot tub turned on the spigot to add another 200 gallons of cold water to the steaming-hot hot tub until the mixture was just right.

Every time I went to the outhouse, I said a little personal prayer, which I called "Prayer at the Outhouse." I'd sit down on the privy and look up at the mountain where the spring was and relax my sphincters.

Water returns to water,
from which it has never been separated.

I saw, I imagined the water traveling from mountain (not me), through pipes (not me), through a faucet (not me), into my water bottle (not me), into my mouth (still not me yet), into my body where it turned into saliva, blood, lymph, mucus, tears, digestive juices, and urine.

An hour or two later, I sat, passing water in the outhouse (definitely not me). The water that passed through me returned to the mountain from which it came, just a hundred yards away. Was the urine passing out of my body "me"? Was that water "mine"?

I passed water out of my body and it flowed right back into the mountain from which it came. Was the water ever different?

After a few days, all the water in my 70 percent water body was from that spring on that mountain. All the air in my body was from the breeze and the wind off the ocean. The heat in my body was from the California sun. The lack of heat was from the coolness, sometimes coldness, of the wind. "My" inner heat came from composting food eaten right there on the Lost Coast.

The food had been flown in on a Cessna, and the cook in the kitchen prepared it all right there on the spot.

During our silent meals, eaten outdoors, I noticed the hardness of food, a.k.a. the earth element, in my mouth. After a few chews, the tongue held the food, and I swallowed the water that had been pressed out of the food by my teeth. Eating became an exercise in noticing earth, water, and heat, or lack of heat.

The next line of my "Prayer at the Outhouse" was

Earth returns to earth,
from which it has never been separate.

The earth element in the body is the slowest to be replaced. Since all the cells in our bodies change every seven years, possibly my cells contain traces of every meal I've eaten in the past few years. Possibly my cells contain traces of earth from all the countries, all the places my food has come from. All that food, going in through the mouth, digested by juices, composted by the body, and then excreted at the outhouse.

So, here's my question: Where was I from?

My 70 percent water body was from the Lost Coast. All the air in my body was from the Lost Coast. The heat in my body? Generated by food eaten on the Lost Coast.

My mind would say I am from the places I hold in my memories—the house I grew up in, the places where I went to school, my home with Bill in Vermont.

But what would my body say? My body during those two weeks was "from" the Lost Coast.

I am home
in the here and the now.

EXPIRATION DATE

Shelf Life

W HEN MY FATHER died at very nearly the same age as did his next older brother, I began to wonder if people—their bodies, that is—have a shelf life. When Dad's caboose brother saw that three of his older brothers had expired either right before or right after their eightieth birthdays, he saw the handwriting on the wall. Unkies didn't take care of his diabetic body and took the express train out of his weary, obese life, expiring just two weeks before his seventy-fourth birthday. His mother, who had doted on her by-far-the-youngest child, died just after her seventy-fourth birthday, and Unkies' favorite sister, Mary, expired at exactly the same age their mother had: seventy-four years and seven weeks. Do I see a pattern here? Or is it all in my imagination?

I'm thinking about this because I recently saw Cal. Her husband Ken died almost a year ago, and she just returned from his next-younger brother's funeral. When siblings die in the same order they were born in, well, it sounds predetermined to me. Connie's mother died of a heart attack at seventy-four, following in the footsteps of her oldest sister, who also died of a heart attack at age seventy-four. Do you think I'm citing anecdotal examples as evidence?

On the day my mother died, I had been talking to the hospice nurse about how I had tried to soothe my mother, to give her permission to go. "The body unwinds on its own," the nurse said.

Oh. I can neither hurry the process up nor slow it down. I can only witness it.

Nowadays when my friends talk about their latest bodily events, I sympathize but I refrain from opinions such as *Too bad* or *It shouldn't be like that* or *That's not fair.* The body is unwinding on its own schedule.

My friend Catherine was wondering about our mutual friend Linda, who will soon turn eighty. Linda's body is failing faster than Bill's, for instance. Catherine asked if Bill could talk to Linda, but I really don't think that Bill advising Linda on how to be more healthy will help Linda. Yes, Bill just spoke about aging in one of the Keene State College's Friday classes for senior citizens. Bill has his theories about why he still looks and acts younger than eighty; daily exercise, a healthy diet, staying active in the community, volunteering, continuing to work to earn a weekly paycheck by keeping his fingers moving over piano and organ keyboards at various churches.

Bill is quite disciplined; he learned discipline by being what he calls "academically challenged." As hard as he studied in school, he still didn't get it. He barely squeaked through high school. Then he went to the New

England Conservatory and studied piano. He played for hours every day and graduated magna cum laude.

I really don't think Bill can say anything to Linda, who eats healthily and stays active in her community. Simply, her body is unwinding at a different speed than Bill's. Comparisons are really useless, and unasked-for advice of limited value.

My friend Barbara, age sixty-five, has been diagnosed with a chronic kidney disease that will probably trigger other physical failures. I don't like to hear that. I don't like to think that. Her older brother died twenty years ago. Her older sister, diagnosed with hepatitis C, had a liver transplant. Maybe the telomeres on her genes just aren't as long as she and I would like. Barbara exercises; she hikes Monadnock every month of the year—that means micro-spikes on the ice of December, January, February. Barbara eats organic food. She does community service. Yet her body goes through its own process, beginning its winding down—which, I hope, will take years and years or even a couple of decades.

Of course, no one knows their own expiration date for sure, though Connie and her four siblings take age seventy-four very seriously. Her oldest brother turns seventy-four this year, and, although there may be quite a lot of teasing and joking among the five of them, there's also a feeling of waiting for the other shoe to drop. This year? Or not?

Our expiration date approaches.

Turning Sixty

My youngest brother, Beau, turned sixty in January 2015. He delights in being the youngest, rubbing in the fact that his three older siblings are *old*—we're all in our sixties. I turned sixty-seven the month before Beau turned sixty, Dona is sixty-five; Paul is sixty-three. And now Beau joins us in the sixties decade.

When Bill turned sixty, I gave him a *New York Times* article about sixty being the gift decade. You still have your health, or most of it. Family responsibilities have lightened up and, for some, work responsibilities are lightening up as well. In your sixties, you can focus on what you want to do. You can retire and be busier than you ever were while you were working. Bill is nineteen years older than Beau, so I can safely say that, at seventy-nine, Bill has had two gift decades—his sixties and his seventies.

When my brother Paul turned sixty, he sighed, "I don't want to be o-l-d." Even though he's independently wealthy, he still is up at five thirty and working outdoors all day long, starting at seven. He's still driving and repairing heavy equipment—backhoes, bulldozers, and dump trucks—just as he's done since Dad put him on a tractor at age five.

Even though I still have energy and stamina, my looks are fading fast. I didn't realize I should have had all my beauty shots taken at fifty-nine, because it's been a fast downhill for the face since then. I look old even though I don't feel old. Goodbye estrogen means goodbye to the body's natural lubricants. Some women wrinkle faster and more deeply than others. That would be me. Oh, sigh.

I used to think women lost their looks while men retained theirs, but this isn't true, either. I'm surprised by how many men my age look my age. Bill retains enough collagen in his face that he looks younger than I do. Only his silvery-white hair gives him away.

So now my youngest brother is sixty. That means that he's old, but it also means that *I'm* old. It's hard to believe. On the one hand, it's just a number, and on the other hand, it's a countdown to some unforeseeable end. How many chapters does my book have? Seventy-four? Eighty-five? Ninety-two? I don't really need to know, and I wouldn't skip ahead to find out even if I could.

For now, my brother and I tease each other about being old, and we compare how our genes are aging. And, for now, life is robust.

Loss of Energy

IN MID-APRIL, I came down with a respiratory
something or other and lay on the sofa for a week,
napping. I completely lost my energy, my oomph, my
get-up-and-go. After a week, the deep cough softened
into something occasional, soft, and loose, but I continued to take four naps a day. I had lost my appetite. Nothing sounded good. I lost my appetite for life. What's the
use, anyway?

My ego floated off a little way. I didn't want to do
anything except look off into space or sleep. My usual
busyness of finishing taxes, editing my writing, and
gardening all lost their appeal. Mostly, I lay on the sofa,
looking out the window, looking at the sky, and desiring
nothing—no food, nothing to do, nothing to read, nothing. Life was this, then—nothing. I felt like my ninety-
four-year-old hospice client, who is not interested in
anything and only wants to sleep.

The first week, my body ached. I felt old, and I
wondered if I would ever be able to exercise again. After
a week, the aches went away. Ahhh. A pain-free body
never felt so good.

After the second week, I began to have a few hunger

pangs for particular foods, though it would take another week before I actually cooked something.

Bill thought I was somatic. *Moi*. The one who is so quick to point out how Bill's body somaticizes his experience, how his body says something he could never say out loud.

Well, he did have a point. This lack of energy corresponded exactly with my tenants sending me accusatory letters and eventually hateful emails about what a despicable person I am. They moved out with two weeks' notice, and I suddenly felt much better.

I, who pride myself on being strong, on being self-reliant, on being able to cope and to deal—well, maybe I'm not as good at that as I want to be. If I believed in voodoo dolls, I might actually wonder if someone had been sticking pins in my effigy or working some sort of black magic.

I kept trying to practice my own white magic of positivity, of hardwiring happiness, of forgiveness. I trotted out the temporary salve of self-talk: "Victims are violent people." Oh, yes. A victim (my tenant) needs a rescuer to rescue her from the persecutor (that would be me). The would-be rescuer doesn't see that she and the victim collude to persecute the persecutor. It's up to me not to fall into the victim role and thereby keep the triangle going.

The positivity that worked best for me was gratitude. "Thank goodness those tenants moved out. They gave only two weeks' notice, but now they have another place to live. Thank God!"

I tried not to focus on the fact that I had to hire a lawyer to deal with the tenants, something I have never before had to do. The good thing about the lawyer was that I had someone on my team. I didn't have to be the bad guy all by myself. The lawyer could write the letter with muscle and authority. I had already tried writing innocuous and placating emails to the tenants, and received only vitriol in response. Time to let the professional take care of things.

Two weeks after they moved out, for the first time, I could actually wish the ex-tenants well in their new life; in part, that's due to the joy I cultivate. By flooding my emotions with other joys, those little stickpins of the tenant story lose their power. Forgiveness becomes a reality when I no longer believe the story that I have about my ex-tenants—a remedy for the soul as well as the body. I even forget the hateful and bullying word the husband called me; I literally cannot remember it.

Energy returned, I'm ready to start eating again, ready to resume my gardening and writing life.

Decade by Decade

BILL IS EIGHTY-ONE, but I tell him that his sixties lasted almost all the way through his seventies. The sixties are a time when you still have your energy, and when you can work if you wish or work toward the purpose of your life. You still have enough health to go and do and laugh and play, even though you've started taking a daily medication for a chronic disease.

Just past his seventy-ninth birthday, Bill started itching. Six months later he slipped on a trail, severed his quadriceps tendon, and had emergency knee surgery the next day. That's when I would say he truly entered into his seventies—when he was seventy-nine. So now he's eighty-one, but he acts and looks like someone ten years younger, and he is still not taking any daily meds. But two years later, he's still itching, maybe because of a nickel allergy, which he seems to be able to control through diet. He's still working, playing the organ twice a week for two churches, and that seems to keep him young. Earning $200 a week, he has a purpose: he likes being able to send each of his daughters a few thousand dollars every year.

My friend Susan is seventy-one, and has had pancreatic cancer for eight years. She's just now going into hospice care—as soon as she gets home from the hospital, that is. Chronologically, she's seventy-one, but I would say she entered her seventies maybe ten years ago, with her second bout of cancer. Now that this five-foot-ten-inch woman weighs ninety-five pounds, she's in her eighties or even nineties, and soon we will say farewell to her in this lifetime.

I myself am sixty-nine, but I'm wondering if I'm entering my seventies a bit early. My body is not quite as old as Bill's, but maybe I'm not that much younger than he is, either, despite what our birth certificates say.

The seventies seem to have a little less energy than the sixties—maybe just one event, one appointment a day. There's not quite as much going and doing. Life slows down a little bit. By this time, you've had a knee or hip replacement. Friends are dropping all around you, yet you are left standing, and you're not sure why. Somewhere around mid-decade, there's an emergency trip to the hospital for the heart, a TIA, a little something from which you easily recover—yet you know you're being put on notice. If you're still traveling, it's a time for cruises and guided tours.

The eighties? Now you know you are on the downhill slide. It's time to start closing up shop and to downsize. In your eighties, you stop driving at night. Due to some hospitalization, your weight drops. There's not quite as much of the "you" as there used to be. You look like a thinner, paler version of yourself.

Although they don't notice, the sixty-somethings

start touching handrails on stairs. By their seventies, people are grasping and holding on to the handrail. The eighty-somethings are not only holding onto handrails but also to other pieces of furniture as they cross the room. I watched one retired farmer, the same age as Bill, hold onto the chair in front of him as he stood to speak at a community meeting. This unsteadiness is due to sarcopenia—the loss of muscle mass. Eighty-year olds don't sit down in a chair; they plop, because their leg muscles aren't strong enough to hold them up on the way down.

Several ninety-year-old friends have moved to assisted living or moved in with a daughter. Now it's time to take it easy, stop the volunteer work, and lead a smaller, narrower life.

Of course, these developmental decades have little to do with actual chronological age. Sometimes we spend but a few years in a decade, rushing on ahead of our peer group to the inevitable.

Seventy-one-year-old Susan is quickly flowing ahead of her peer group, sailing down the river to join the ocean. Meanwhile, Bill has been dallying in the shallows, caught in the eddies along the shore, glorying in the vanity and vitality of his still-fit body.

Labeling Furniture

Now that Bill has entered his eighties, I am really trying not to take our life together for granted. It's so easy to live day to day, doing our normal things, following our usual schedules, having our little tiffs that come and go like smoke. I try to practice being grateful for his companionship, yet ordinary days pass by as if the two of us are going to go on like this forever. He's at an age where, for every two years he lives, his life expectancy increases by one year. He tells me he has less than 10 percent of his life remaining. There's only one gallon of gas left in his tank.

My financial planner expects me to live to ninety-two—that's twenty-three more years, which is sort of scary. That could be fifteen years without Bill, so my gas tank is supposedly a quarter full. On the one hand, I'm confident that I can "do" it. I was single for twenty years before I met Bill, so being alone isn't the part that bothers me. It's being alone after having had thirty years of companionship. Missing someone who knows me so thoroughly and loves me despite that.

Of course, Life might have a few tricks up her sleeve. Maybe I will die before Bill. While I was on my

February retreat at home, Bill asked me to write him a letter detailing what he should do in case I die first. In addition to that five-page letter, I went around the house and stuck labels on the backs of paintings and the undersides of furniture designating whom they should go to.

My friend Delia says that some of the stuff she inherited from her grandmother still has a square light spot where her grandmother had applied labels designating who was to get what.

I keep unloading stuff. I've passed most of my heirlooms (sentimental tchotchkes) on to nieces and nephews. All I have left are my mother's paintings. Bill is the one who has real heirlooms—Tiffany glassware, the complete set of his grandfather's silverware, furniture—that he passes on to his daughter at the rate of one piece every year or two.

With the letter written, the furniture labeled, life goes on as if everything is normal. Can I feel grateful for Bill in every moment that I remember to? One of these days, either he or I will no longer be here with the other one. All the stuff that decorates our lives will belong to someone else. My idea of "home"—this particular home that Bill and I share—will evaporate into thin air. Where did it go? It's a mystery. All I know for sure is that every place I have ever called "home" is gone. Every person that I have lived with—parents, siblings, friends, roommates, lovers—is now either past tense or far away. Gone. Just like my collection of stuff.

Esther's Butternuts

Our county forester, Bill Guenther, keeps track of all the biggest trees in our county. My friend Beverly, who lives in Brattleboro, called him because she thought she might have the biggest mulberry tree. The largest Japanese maple in the county, and in the state, grows in the backyard of the B&B at 40 Putney Road.

Several years ago, my neighbor Esther, who lived in a 200-year-old farmhouse in the middle of what used to be acres of fields on top of a hill, called Bill Guenther to come look at her butternut tree. A butternut tree, also called a white walnut, looks quite similar to a black walnut tree. Walnut trees, like goldenrod, are allelopathic, meaning that their roots emit a toxin that kills off any competitor trying to grow nearby. There, on top of the hill, with a 360-degree view, stood the queen of the meadow, all by herself—Esther's spreading butternut tree, twice as wide as she was tall.

The county forester measured it this way and that. Yes, it was the biggest butternut tree in the county, and it turned out to be the biggest butternut tree in the state.

In her eighties and nineties, Esther lived from month

to month on her Social Security. One of the dozen ways she kept herself busy and useful in life was to find someone who could use the gazillions of butternuts that her tree produced every year. Marty Collins, retired from the Putney post office, gathered up a truckload, off-loaded them onto a concrete pad, let them dry there, then ran over them with his truck, back and forth to crack them open. He gathered up that mess, mashed it into a slurry in an old concrete mixer, and then sold the butternut mash as seed.

Esther was fascinated by the process, happy to have her lawn cleaned up, and amazed that her butternut might have some sort of global reach.

On January 31, 2015, ninety-four-year-old Esther was found dead in her driveway with a smile on her lips. The coroner's report said "heart attack." She'd had a cow's valve put in ten years earlier, and the life expectancy of those valves is ten years. She had been a nurse. She knew.

But if she had some seconds, some minute before she lost consciousness, perhaps she lay there in her driveway looking up at the blue sky and smiling at her now-bare butternut tree.

Esther's Death

THE CORONER'S REPORT said that Esther died of a heart attack, and quickly. That's a comforting story for the bereaved, but what if that's not quite the way it happened?

After my father died, I found an open, empty bottle of sleeping pills by his bedside. When the doctor called to tell us that, sight unseen, he was putting "congestive heart failure" on Dad's death certificate, I took the phone into Dad's bedroom, closed the door, and asked about the empty bottle.

A year before, Dad had asked me if I would give him a little white pill when the time came, and I'd said, "Yes—if you get the agreement of my siblings." I didn't know that he'd already asked my evangelical brother, who had said "No."

Had Dad taken his little white pill himself? I wouldn't put it past him. Still, I felt a bit shaken to consider the possibility that Dad had hurried his dying process along.

"Do you want me to do an autopsy?" the doctor asked.

"Oh, no!" I said. "I'm just trying to come to peace with this myself."

"His heart failed," said the doctor.

"Okay, thanks," I said.

That's a much better story for public consumption. I would have said, "His kidneys failed"—but they had failed five years earlier, and Dad had been living with them and dying from them ever since.

Esther was driving out her driveway on January 31. Her car stopped. She got out of the car. She walked with a wide stance as if she had neuropathy, as if she had lost the nerves in her feet. Let's say she slipped on the icy snow on that ten-degree day. What if Esther fell down in her driveway on Friday afternoon and couldn't get up? She tried to crawl toward her house, 200 feet away, but soon gave that up. Maybe the heart attack happened then? Or maybe she saw death coming. Just one minute, two minutes ago, she had walked out of her house, backed the car out of the garage, on her way to do an errand. Her next good deed, an egg custard for a sick friend, sat cooling on her kitchen counter. She followed her driveway as it bent left. Then she stopped the car. Or the car stopped and wouldn't go any farther? Now, life had taken two left-hand turns she hadn't been expecting: a clunked-out car, her own fall on the driveway. And now, now, perhaps Death was walking across the snowy field or sneaking out of the pine woods behind her so that she couldn't quite see him, or perhaps sitting there under the spreading butternut tree, slowly standing up and stretching his long limbs as he turned to gaze at her.

Those of us of sound mind and body can still run

away from the thought, the smell, the sight, the touch of death, avert our eyes, turn our heads, plug our ears, and sing *la-la-la* so that we can't hear the last gasp of life—that precious final breath. For the open, for the vulnerable—for Esther—there was a blue sky, the feel of frozen wind on her cheeks, and an oh-so-familiar loss of self. She'd lost herself after she'd broken her hip, and it took a few disconcerting months of rehab to find her self again.

And now, her self had gone missing again. Life reclaiming her as part of *it*self. So, this is what people call Death?

She smiled.

CPSIA information can be obtained
at www.ICGtesting.com
Printed in the USA
FFOW05n1648101217